THE CO-AUTHOR

LIAM HAYES has followed the Irish rugby team through the Five Nations championship and written about the game since 1986. He is a former Sportswriter of the Year for his work on boxing and athletics, and he was Chief Sports Features Writer with THE SUNDAY PRESS for nine years.

His journalistic career went hand-in-hand with a Gaelic football career, and in 1987 and '88 he was a midfielder on the Meath team which won All-Ireland Senior Football championships. He captained Meath in the 1991 All-Ireland final. He is married, with two children, and lives in Lucan, Co. Dublin.

POPPY

TIME TO RUCK AND ROLL

Nick Popplewell

with

Liam Hayes

Published in Ireland by
HERO BOOKS
Lucan
Co. Dublin

© HERO BOOKS 1995
0 9526260 0 4

Cover photograph: Sportsfile
Section one photographs: Sportsfile
Section two photographs: Inpho

Printed by Colorprint Ltd., Dublin.
Design & Origination: Treadstone International Ltd., Leixlip.

for Mum & Dad
and Rachel

CONTENTS

A WORD FROM TNT EXPRESS WORLDWIDE

TNT Express Worldwide are delighted to sponsor 'Poppy: Time to Ruck and Roll'. It is a revealing book which will greatly interest rugby fans and sporting-minded people everywhere.

When TNT was invited to sponsor this book I was quickly sold by Nick Popplewell's enthusiasm and love for the game which he graces with such skills, plus his determination not to pull any punches where he feels hard-hitting or controversial comment is necessary.

TNT is a worldwide organisation which has built a global reputation for getting involved and helping out in all types of sports. From sponsoring referees' kits on the rugby fields of Australia to the tracksuits of the Cup final winners at Wembley Stadium, the TNT brand is to be seen promoting sport for the benefit of all nations and all communities. We try to be sports-minded and community-minded, and as caring corporate citizens we do our best to put something back into the societies in which we live. Here, in Ireland, TNT already sponsors European double gold medallist, Michelle Smith, but in addition to swimming we have substantial sponsorships in soccer (Finn Harps F.C.), rugby (Dolphin R.F.C.), basketball (Killester B.C., K.P. Coasters) and many other sports. There are only two major exceptions, Gaelic football and hurling, and it is our commitment to pursue sponsorship in both sports in the near future.

I would like to pay tribute to all the TNT staff here in Ireland for making the company a winner.

TNT Express Worldwide is a young, successful, vibrant company, associated with speed and achievement by the very nature of its business. Consequently, our association with sport and, in particular Nick Popplewell's autobiography, is all the more relevant and important. In conclusion, to Nick we wish continued success on the rugby field. To our readers, I hope you enjoy this book as much as I have. TNT is delighted to have played a part in bringing this publication to you.

Happy reading!

Geoff Carr,
Managing Director,
TNT Express Worldwide,
Ireland.

ACKNOWLEDGEMENTS

On a rainy London evening, last January, Liam Hayes and I decided to write this book. The long, hot World Cup in South Africa was still several months away, and there was little hint that by the end of the year rugby would have officially said goodbye to amateurism, but Liam convinced me that 1995 was going to be a big year for the old game. He was right.

While the book is presented as an autobiography, 'Poppy' also has one foot in the past and one foot in the future. The same as the Irish rugby team, actually! In the pages ahead I hope that people can enjoy the old days (defeats included), and look forward to years in which the Irish rugby team will hopefully share the pitch with the world's best and genuinely think of winning, every game, every day.

I want to thank Liam Hayes for being more than my side-kick in this book. The Irish rugby team, I also have to thank, I suppose! We have had some hard times in the '90s. Good times too! They are a good bunch of boys who have given an awful lot to the game. I hope that this book does them justice.

A great many other rugby players and coaches, officials, doctors and physios also have to be thanked for helping me down through the years, on Lions and Baabaas teams, Irish and Leinster teams, Greystones and Gorey teams. Not forgetting Wasps in the last 12 months. Without all of them, there would be no book.

I am thankful to Greystones for each of the nine years I spent with that fantastic club. Without all my old team-mates and old friends, and their constant encouragement and support, there might have been no Ireland and Lions for me.

I am indebted to Anne McSweeney in the union for her tireless work on behalf of the Irish players, Ned Van Esbeck for his faith in Irish rugby through good times and bad, and Brian Hurson for seeing to it that this prop would scrummage for another few years.

TNT Express Worldwide have offered me encouragement and valuable support in the creation of this book, and with the support of Geoff Carr, Veronica O'Connell and the people in T.N.T., Liam Hayes and I were able to clear all hurdles.

Lastly, I thank my mother and father, my three 'big' brothers and my kid brother, David.

And, most importantly, to Rachel, my wife, a big thank-you!

FOREWORD

Playing for Ireland means the world to me. The green jersey, No. 1 on my back, the noise and the sight of Lansdowne Road! I dreamed about it for years!

In the last few years of my life, however, those dreams of wearing the green shirt and hearing the crowd roar at Lansdowne Road all around me have threatened to spill over into nightmares. Though, thankfully, I can say I have always avoided waking up in a sweaty state on the morning of an International game. The morning after an International game? That's a whole different story.

The Irish rugby team has been insulted and abused hundreds of times in recent years. Some of the great players I have played with walked to an early retirement, wondering if playing for Ireland was worth it?

It is sad that any sportsman who has sacrificed the best years of his life, should be driven to having to ask such a question.

We are a great people. We have huge hearts. And we love to shout and cheer, and we love to have a drink in celebration. We also love to criticise at times, and that is everybody's right. But it would be a great tragedy if the day ever arrived when rugby in Ireland was to be ripped apart in an angry and maddening effort to reach the heart of the game.

Rugby is a big-hearted game. It has served this country brilliantly for a long, long time, and it has always been able to stride across religious and political divides. Rugby is a very important game in this country.

In deciding to write this book, I wanted to offer up a personal, honest, hopefully amusing, hopefully surprising, but true account of the life of an Irish rugby player. I know it is something unusual for an Irish rugby player to do while he is still trotting out onto Lansdowne Road.

Usually players wait until they are 10 years down the retirement road before putting pen to paper.

But the time is right, in my opinion, for an Irish rugby player to now speak up. Just a few months ago I played in the World Cup finals in South Africa, which were a fantastic success, but the tournament proved beyond any shadow of a doubt that the game at International level is now moving almost at the speed of lightning. And I don't mean just on the rugby field!

On the field and off the field, rugby players are now thinking, behaving and preparing in the same way as athletes in every other professional sport in the world. In reaching the quarter-finals of the World Cup last Summer, the Irish team showed that it has the ability and the commitment necessary to follow the strongest International teams down the path they have chosen for themselves and the game.

Last August, in Paris, rugby union said goodbye to amateurism. It is now time for every country to start afresh. And it is time for a country like Ireland to start making up some ground. We have been off the pace for a long time. We have been lapped by some countries. At times, we looked to be in a bad state. But, now, Ireland has an opportunity to get back into the race. I hope we are soon up and running.

I sincerely hope that this book will help Irish players, administrators and supporters to see, a little bit more clearly, what we have to do.

My own feeling is that it is time to get stuck into the game, and forget about the past if we have to! It is time to give a decent account of ourselves in every single game we play. Time to ruck and roll.

Nick Popplewell,

September, 1995.

CHAPTER 1

EIGHTEEN AND A HALF MINUTES

On a Saturday afternoon back in November, 1989, I raced as fast as my short little legs would take me onto the International rugby stage for the first time. The place was Lansdowne Road. The team at the opposite end of the ground, sharing the billing with Ireland, was the All Blacks.

It appeared to be the perfect start. Lansdowne Road, the All Blacks, and yours truly in the green No.1

Eighteen and a half minutes later, Nicholas James Popplewell - that's me - had his International rugby career come to a sudden grinding halt and in front of 50,000 people at Lansdowne Road and zillions more watching the game on television, I was slowly led back to the sideline and into the Irish dressing room after cracking two ribs in a scrum.

Now you see me, now you don't! I was 25 years-old, and who would have thought that two cracked ribs would cost me almost two years of International rugby? It wasn't fair, and it definitely did not make sense, but this country is littered with half-decent and fairly decent rugby players who once got their nose into the Irish dressing room, and then had the door slammed closed on them.

That is one of the great faults with Irish rugby. We open doors too easily and close them far too quickly, and lots of players only end up with one International cap to plonk on their head for the rest of their life. I was luckier than some others. I was not going to allow people to forget about me. It's bad enough being a one cap wonder, but eighteen and a half minutes would have been bloody ridiculous.

It was, however, a great, fantastic, totally enjoyable eighteen and a half minutes, and I can definitely understand how players who have only played for Ireland once still feel that they have experienced just about everything in their careers.

Willie Anderson was Irish captain that afternoon. And I, unfortunately, was linked close to Willie as we were facing the Haka. So I ended up about three or four inches from Wayne Shelford's teeth. It was the heat of the moment, and it was the huge emotion generated by shouting back at the All Blacks as they did their thing, which brought Willie across the halfway line and into Shelford's face.

Looking back, our action was disrespectful, but at the time we thought that linking arms and confronting them might help us to perform. We ended up losing the game 23-6 and it was not a bad Irish performance. As they shouted and made fists at us, I'm not sure what I was thinking about.

I was not petrified, but I was extremely apprehensive. What were we shouting back at them? I honestly still have absolutely no idea what it was. Everything was happening so fast. We met the President, there was the Haka, and I was off injured. Just like that! It was an awful disappointment, even though I kicked the ball a few times in those eighteen and a half minutes and I put in two or three tackles.

It had taken me so long to get selected for that game, years of hard work, and bang! I'm gone for two years! People started to talk about me not being able to scrummage. Total rubbish, but the word spread and some people wouldn't shut up about it.

I watched the rest of the game from the sideline, and I delayed going to the hospital until the Sunday afternoon. I didn't want to go on the Saturday night. I drank a few pints. I was on pain-killers. To be honest I drank more than a few pints before the night was over. Ribs or no ribs, I collapsed into bed in the end and I slept my head off.

My first International appearance was not the sort of arrival and exit I would have wished for, but I had at last tasted the good, hard, punishing life. And, believe me, it is a great life.

The front row of an International rugby team is an educational and interesting place to spend a few years, and you do bump into quite a variety of different, amusing and sometimes dangerous people. Luckily, you also end up with the biggest bunch of friends you could ever have hoped to have.

You end up in a room full of good mates, and with a few psychos thrown in just to keep things interesting. That's what the front row is, it's a private members' club! I'm in there at the moment, wearing Philly Orr's old shirt, and somebody else will take the No.1 shirt from me when my time is up, though I would like to think I have another two or three years left.

I am not a naturally hard or particularly ruthless person. I didn't chew on bricks in my younger days or use six inch nails as tooth-picks, but I know what has to be done on the field. I know what is expected of me, and if I have to be the hard man I will be the hard man. I will do it. So too will Terry Kingston, Keith Wood, Peter Clohessy, Gary Halpin or any of the Irish players I am closest to, though having said that, I have to admit that there is not one everyday, naturally hard man in the Irish squad at present apart from Davy Tweed.

There's nobody around anymore like Willie Duggan, who did not tolerate any fooling around or messing from opposing teams. Very few teams tried it on with Ireland, and got away with it, when Duggan was there. With me, if I am thumped during the match, then I will take care of the situation myself, but some of the younger players do not know what to do sometimes. Every International team needs somebody on the field looking after the younger and inexperienced player, and that's what Ireland have lacked in recent years.

There are, however, tough men on the Irish team who can deter opposing players without having to do too much. Clohessy, or the Claw as he is fondly known, is one tough man. The story of him, on his back, floating out to sea during Ireland's tour of Australia two years ago, with the rest of the Irish team standing on the beach looking at him disappearing between waves, is one which sums up The Claw appropriately. 'If de Claw bumps into any of dem sharks,' muttered somebody, 'there'll be an awful row!'

Fewer players are brutally taken out of the game anymore, which is a good thing. The game at International level has become so fast, even in recent years, that there is little time for any real nastiness anymore.

Referees and linesmen are also less tolerant than they used to be and that has also led to a reduction in the number of cheap shots during games. It's a good thing, though there will always be occasional outbursts. I had to throw a few digs at Phil Davies when we played Wales last season, but it was in the heat of the moment. I saw him involved with one of our boys, and I felt it was up to me to step in.

But, nowadays, there are very few players on the field looking to break another player's jaw or cheekbone. The penalties are too great for that sort of behaviour. A whole year can be over if a player is caught in one stupid act and, worse still, with the legal situation as it now stands in relation to sports injuries a player could get six months, in jail, if he is not careful in future. And that is the way it should be in my opinion.

The game is hard and punishing enough, as it stands, without the cowboys and thugs doing their little bit on the side. In the front row, there is always a confrontation awaiting you. There is always another scrum around the corner. The power and impact involved in scrummaging has the hooker and his two props careering into the equivalent of a stone wall most of the time.

Last year, for instance, I had a slight problem with my neck, a few days before we played England in Twickenham and I needed to have some x-rays taken. The results showed that I had suffered ten or eleven whiplash injuries, which was all news to me. My doctor informed me that most props would have very similar x-ray results to show.

A human being is not naturally designed for the violent impact which is now witnessed when two sets of front rows lock horns. We take a lot of criticism and slagging for the way in which we trot and waddle around the field following the play sometimes, but it seldom dawns on the person sitting in the stand that the poor prop forward in the green shirt is after having a row with a couple of other hippos, and that the unfortunate creature is probably going to be tired and dazed for a few seconds.

Nobody knows what happens in the scrum. I mean nobody on the outside, and that includes the referee most of the time! It is a total law unto itself. It is always being said, for instance, that a team will never collapse a scrum camped on its opponent's goalline. But want to bet? A little nudge-on from the attacking team can collapse it in a second. The referee is human, and he can be fooled. And few referees have ever been prop forwards. Within the scrum you have a fair idea of what is happening around you and, occasionally, you can talk. I might talk to Claw. I used to talk to Dessie Fitzgerald. In the World Cup in South Africa I talked to Gary Halpin, sometimes to upset the other team and sometimes just to get things moving.

Most of the time, especially early on in games, you are concentrating on your position, on your head and your legs, and there may not be time to open your mouth. Next thing the ball is in, and it's gone! The head to head combat might only last for two or three seconds, unless it is a totally defensive scrum or you are going for a pushover try.

The game is changing however and, where once there was anything up to 30 scrums in a game, nowadays there might be only ten or fifteen. The game has changed in the last six years since that November day against the All Blacks.

Richard Loe was the man I came face to face with that day, and if I wasn't in such awful pain as I was being helped away, I probably would have seen him smiling to himself. Eighteen and a half minutes! Loe was a rough, tough cookie, and not the nicest person to meet in the darkness of the scrum. But then he is not told to be!

In 1992, in the first test match of Ireland's tour of New Zealand, I made it one-all with Richard. After 25 minutes he had to leave the field with a leg injury and naturally I was not too concerned about his state of health. That left us at one scalp each!

Richard Loe's disciplinary record makes for interesting reading and in the front row private members' club, not too many of us would ever be queuing up to buy him a feed of drink. Though he is a very good player, and a hard, hard man.

That first day in the Irish shirt I remember shoeing him in the opening couple of minutes. He was on the ground and he didn't deserve any mercy, because if the situation was reversed he would not be stopping to say a prayer over me. Even though I was playing my first game for Ireland, I was smart enough to know that. We had a few words. We warned each other, and I think I told him to fuck off with himself or something like that. Probably did, though shortly after that I was the one who headed off. Out of sight.

On the present All Blacks team Robin Brooke is a tough player. Whereas his brother, Zinzan, is more athletic at No.8 and covers a lot of ground, Robin is generally in the thick of things. If you are messing around with them or doing something you should not be doing, then Robin Brooke will not think twice about sorting it out. Though the All Blacks have hard, strong players all over the field. Frank Bunce, for instance, is well able to look after himself. Generally speaking, there is not a New Zealander who ever needs a minder.

In England, if I was to pick out one player who knows how to stand up for himself and his team it is Dean

Richards. He is a great player, and he is also a strong, strong man. Mickey Skinner was another English player who earned himself a lot of respect from opposing teams. He took what he got on the field, but if he did he saw to it that the punishment was returned with interest. Peter Winterbottom would not take any crap either.

There are fewer Australians who qualify under the 'hard man' title. Willie Ofahengaue, of course, is not somebody you would ever care to have cross words with, though that is exactly what happened at the beginning of Ireland's World Cup quarter-final against Australia in 1991. Philip Matthews and Willie started off with a few digs each, and Franno got thumped by Willie at the end of the little mill. In between, I got a fierce belt from Willie and I was concussed for the rest of the game.

Most of the Australians are gentlemen, though good players! John Eales, for example, does not get too involved unless it is very necessary and Eales is a world class player! Obviously you do not have to be a hard man to be a great player.

The Aussies are on the quiet side, but the French have it in their nature to get hot-headed over a rugby match. French rugby is real 'Beauty and the Beast' stuff, with an awful lot of beasts running around the place.

At home, in Ireland, the hard, punishing games of rugby are usually played in Munster. It follows that they have a larger number of tougher men than most of the other provinces. At the beginning of my career I was always in awe going down to Limerick to play, but I grew to enjoy it and welcome it. It is such an intimidating environment most of the time.

Rugby pitches in Limerick normally double-up as battlefields. Every time you walk off the pitch you know you have played for the full 80 minutes. It is not a safe place to ever put your feet up!

It's warfare, but if you give it back to a Munster team then they will always respect you. In the bar afterwards, there is a great atmosphere usually. A team like Young Munster fully represent Munster rugby at its aggressive best.

Jim Glennon and Dessie Fitzgerald were two of the father-figures in Leinster rugby during my early years in Greystones. They were two players who knew how to lay down the law on the field if the match was getting out of hand. Two big, strong and fiercely respected men!

In recent years, Dean Oswald of Blackrock became a player with a big physical presence, even though he is not a particularly big man. Dean is a New Zealander and you know he will be there when things get rough and tough. The last time I played against him, I recall we threw a few digs at one another in the heat of the moment. Brent Pope, another New Zealander who played for years with St. Mary's, also would put his life on the line most Saturday afternoons.

When Davy Tweed played against France last season in the championship he proved he was more than a tough-looking cookie when he got stuck into Olivier Merle, their huge lock. The two of them getting to grips with one another was not pretty, but Merle found his match in Tweedy and that does not happen every day of the week. Quiet off the field, Tweedy does not suffer fools gladly on it. Speaking as a prop forward, I have to confess that Munster rugby is often my favourite rugby. Someone like Pat O'Hara is one of my very favourite players, though it is wrong to single out any one player in the crowd down there.

I grew to relish playing Young Munster, however, most

of all. In the early years myself and the Claw (Peter Clohessy) would have a private battle all day long. He was not on the Irish team at that stage and I was just getting there. So we both wanted to prove something to whoever was watching. And we also wanted to badly prove something to one another.

For years I did not speak to the Claw. Our battle, I suppose, had turned very personal and that should not have been the case. In the bar, after the match, there would not be a word between us. Then, two years ago, we both ended up on the Irish team together. We ended up rooming together. And for the first time we saw one another as human beings. Our seven-years war ended there and then. When you are playing in the front row for Ireland with somebody, you are virtually depending on them for your life. You have to put the past well behind. Also, wives begin to meet up at that point and that also helps to bring players together more off the pitch.

Nowadays, Claw and myself are friends and I am sure we will be friends for life. I would not think twice of asking him for a few quid if I was short or asking him for a lift somewhere if I was stuck. And he would not think twice either before helping me out. I hope!

The Claw is one Irish player who puts a huge physical effort into his game. It is about half his game, always getting stuck in! Making life as hard as possible for the opposing team! He also gets a hiding at times himself, but it is all in the game with him. It is not a game for the fainthearted.

CHAPTER 2

FAT, SLOW AND UGLY?

Thankfully, since I was a kid, I can say I have never felt scared before a game of rugby, never, and I have never worried about getting myself injured. Apart from that, I'm a complete bag of nerves every time I play for Ireland, and I feel no reason to be ashamed or apologetic about that.

If I am sick with nerves, then I know for sure that I am thinking very seriously about the game, and that is a good thing. But it's not only when I'm playing for Ireland that I feel physically sick. Since moving over to London last year, and joining Wasps, I can honestly say there has not been one Courage League game before which I have not had to dart in and out to the toilet several times.

The captain at Wasps, Dean Ryan, would look at me last season as he was giving his final team talk in the dressing room, and he might shake his head or throw his eyes up to the ceiling. It's pure anticipation on my part. It's not fear, and every time I do make a run for it, there's not much down there anyhow, just loads of fluid, and bananas.

With Wasps, I started off on a whole new rugby career in a different country, and in many ways it was like going right back to when I first moved up to Greystones from Gorey to play Leinster senior rugby. At the time that was also venturing into unknown territory, and I would visit the toilet cubicle before most games.

The hardest game I played in in the last twelve months (before Ireland played the All Blacks in the opening game of the World Cup in South Africa last Summer) was for Wasps against Bath in the Courage league. Long before the game kicked-off, I knew it was going to be a hard game for me. In addition to it being a crucial game for us against England's top team, and a team which would be capable of taking on most International sides and giving them a decent game of it, I was expecting to meet the English tight head prop, Victor Ubogu that afternoon.

I had a few things which needed settling with Victor. A couple of matters which needed straightening out. As it turned out, we won the game but Ubogu wasn't playing. He was touring around Hong Kong for some reason.

I like playing against Victor Ubogu because he is a player with a big reputation, but somebody I don't rate all that highly. He has done well for Bath and he has done reasonably well for England, though in my opinion he will never fill Jeff Probyn's boots. I have nothing against him as a rugby player, but off the field last season, after England had beaten Ireland at Lansdowne Road, Ubogu and Brian Moore had an awful lot to say for themselves and I didn't like what I heard.

As I have already said, front rows all over the world are like a private members' club. We have our own little union within the game of rugby union and there are very few props who don't, at the very least, publicly respect one another. I have never slagged off an opposing prop after a game. It's a one-on-one battle. It can be tough and there can be loads of aggravation, but once the final whistle sounds you buy the other man a drink and say good luck to him.

Victor Ubogu may be one of the nicest guys in rugby, for all I know, but he has still to learn the rules. Props do not behave like crybabies! And that's about the only rule there is.

On the Sunday and Monday after the English match last season, when I went back to London for work that week, some of the tabloid newspapers had me headlined as a cheat. Spread over two pages one of them had 'POPPY THE CHEAT!'. I couldn't believe it, because I have great respect for the English players and since the Lions trip to New Zealand two years ago I have become very matey with half a dozen of them. They're a great bunch, and they are thoroughly genuine on and off the field, and probably too gentlemanly for their own good.

Newspaper people were ringing me up and telling me that Victor Ubogu was complaining that my play had been dangerous, and that he could have broken his neck against Ireland. When I heard that, I genuinely did feel like breaking his neck. I had done nothing against England which had been premeditated. All I did was what had to be done at the time. In the scrum that's allowed.

Victor, as far as I was concerned, had been boring in on our hooker, Keith Wood, in the scrums and to stop him from doing that some people would have grabbed him by the shorts. I grabbed him by the leg instead. It sorted the problem out. Because his body position was twisted in the scrum his right leg was up in front of me and I decided to get it in a deadlock grip. That was that.

You would never find Jeff Probyn complaining after a match (two years ago I had to deal with him the same way as I did with Victor) and you would not find me shouting my mouth off either. Even if somebody got a cheap shot at me during a game, I would keep quiet, remember it and make sure to balance the books the very next time I played against him.

Victor must have been spending too much time with Brian Moore, because he is another one who often has a lot to say to journalists about his opponents. England's hooker has always been one of the high profile players in the game. He is always in the newspapers. I had played with Moore in two test matches for the Lions in New Zealand in 1993 and it appeared to me that we understood one another and respected one another by the end of that tour, but after England beat us last year he was complaining publicly about us as well. In fairness, in the past, he has also spoken up on behalf of players when it was necessary. He has the courage to face up to the establishment on important issues. But you do not turn on your fellow players, and he turned on Scotland last year, and us. After that I had no time for him.

In the Irish dressing room, I have never in my life advocated dangerous play, and on the field I abhor the use of the boot when a player is lying helplessly on the ground and can not protect himself. I have never purposely kicked or stamped on any other player, though I confess I am not opposed to giving a few digs when they are called for. Likewise, if I am on the ball on the wrong side of a ruck, I am going to be raked off it and if an opponent is ruining our ball I will do the same to him. That's fair, and the referee is there to see that nobody gets seriously hurt.

Rugby is about an awful lot more than a light, oval ball

on the ground. It's about friendship and respect too, and the game can be all the more enjoyable when you mix that friendship with healthy competition. If, against England, I get my hands on Rob Andrew then I'll try to half-kill him, because I really like the guy and respect him. In the same game, if he tackles me, he is going to try and make sure that I hit the deck hard.

Afterwards we can have a drink, and he can call me a fucking lunatic and I can call him a fucking chancer, and the next day we might phone each other up. On the Tuesday, we'll be down at Wasps training ground in Sudbury together, and that is the way it is supposed to be.

Props, especially, should feel a great loyalty towards one another, and even a fondness if necessary. Olo Brown and Ewen McKenzie are two good friends of mine, and they're from New Zealand and Australia! Victor Ubogu should not think he is anything special or that anybody in a green shirt is out to get him.

Back in 1992, Jeff Probyn and I played for the Barbarians against the Australians, and about an hour or so before the start of the game we were walking the field when I saw McKenzie. I knew him from years back. He was with Dan Crowley whom I actually played with in Australia in 1987, and the four of us started chatting. The Aussies had a few nights of beer in them by then and they had probably played a few rounds of golf, as they waited for the Baa-baas game to be the usual runaround stuff. Anyhow, the four of us agreed that we should enjoy the afternoon. We agreed to go light on each other in all the scrums, but walking back to our dressing room Probyn turns to me and says 'Fuck them!' When the first scrum arrived in the game, we must have shoved them back half a mile. All hell broke loose after that. We tore into each other, and we also had one hell of a night, and a much better night than we would have had had we taken the game easy.

Playing in the front row is a physical, unforgiving game by its very nature. We are banging heads and swiping at each other, and if you were taking everything that happens on a rugby field personally you would not even be talking to half the members of your own team at the end of the game. I have no interest in a Poppy V's Ubogu feud, that's just childish, running to the newspapers! If we were to go down that road, the next thing is you might find me announcing to the world that Victor Ubogu farts in the scrum. Who needs that?

The scrum itself is a place unlike anywhere else. Some days you can feel at home in there, and other days you can be fighting for your life. In many respects it is also a secret place. Most people outside of that moving and steaming mass of human flesh do not have the remotest idea of what exactly is happening in there. That includes all journalists, even those who hint in their match reports that they have their finger on the pulse of the scrum. They rely on guesswork, the same as the supporters.

Basically, a scrummaging unit is simply enough explained. The central objective is for the front five to be stuck to one another. Excuse me, but for best effect, we have got to be like shit to a blanket. The hooker has his arm over my shoulder. I have my right arm around his lower body, grabbing the waistband of his shorts, with my thumb on the inside for a better grip. On a wet day a jersey can stretch forever, so it's better to get the shorts, though some hookers do not like being grabbed by the shorts because it allows them much less movement.

When the two packs meet it is important for me to keep my left arm locked out straight in front of me. If I can grab the tight head prop by his shorts it's fantastic, but the chances are the loose head will not be allowed to reach them. But if I do get his shorts, it means I'm in control, chum!

In our scrum, we want to keep ourselves low and tight, so that our hooker can not be messed around by their tight head. I will have a wide stance, because the ball is going through my legs, and so I'm not in a pushing position as such. That is my basic position in the scrum, but one hundred and one things can happen after that to change the whole picture. At the end of the day, however, it is always one of the props whom Joe Bloggs blames for the scrum being in trouble.

In reality, if there is a problem in the scrum the chances are it is not one of the props. It is quite likely somebody else or something else which happened! The wing forward not doing his job or not being there, or one of the second rows not getting his timing spot on. There are so many other things which dictate what happens in the front row.

It is very hard for somebody at Lansdowne Road, watching from fifty yards away or one hundred yards even, to identify the reason why an Irish scrum is in trouble. I might look bad to some people, because our tight head is being destroyed by his man! Or I might be letting somebody else down! It's difficult to know, and I do not know how referees do their job. To be honest, half the time I think they don't know what is going on and in those cases they observe a few general rules, like the attacking team is never going to collapse a scrum! Referees look for help from the law of averages.

There are referees who are exceptions. Owen Doyle, for example, is one of Ireland's outstanding referees, and in England last year I met several clever refs. When we played Bath in a vital league game, for instance, the scrum collapsed on their ball in front of our posts, and nine out of 10 referees would have penalised Wasps in that situation. But the referee that afternoon knew what was going on and gave the decision to us.

Owen Doyle is a great referee because he does not distance himself from the two teams on the field. He understands players and will even offer them encouragement to do the right thing. And players respond to a referee like that. Against Terenure, a few years back, I remember one instance where I stood on an opponent and everybody in the ground wanted me off. Even the Greystones boys thought I was in big trouble. It had been a complete accident and, before I explained myself to Owen, he told me he understood exactly what had happened, but he also told me not to be an eejit and do anything for the remainder of the game. His approach and the authority he brings to a game demands respect from both teams, which he usually receives.

When most people think of prop forwards they think of poor, squat, tired figures with their jerseys all over the place and their shorts down to their ankles. We do not look good or very athletic, and we definitely do not look very attractive. When people talk about the great games of rugby, and the brilliant tries, the names of very few props crop up in the conversation. We know that. And when videos of games and tries are sold we barely get a look-in.

That's life! People are going to remember Geoghegan and Blanco, Campese and Lomu for years and years, and long after some of the world's greatest props have been forgotten. In 10 years time how many people will be talking about Tony Daly, who scored Australia's only try in the 1991 World Cup final against England? Campese, Horan and Little, Farr-Jones, and Lynagh are going to come before him, and even when the Aussie pack is recalled Ofahengaue, their No.8 and Eales, their second row, are going to beat Daly to it. That is the way it has always been for us poor props, but we have a good sense of humour and a good knowledge of the real game!

It should not be hard for people to understand, therefore, the great respect and loyalty props have for one another. We are in the front line. When the time comes for two teams to go to war we lead the way. At the end of the day, and even at the end of the game, an awful lot of people may have forgotten that, but when prop forwards sit down to dinner together that evening or stand at the bar, we know the real story. There is no game of rugby which is won by a dainty wing flying down the touchline and scoring a try. Usually that is just the finishing touch. The real game is won over 80 minutes, and how can you compare 79 minutes of hard work from a prop and 60 seconds of genius from a winger? You can't, but props know that the 79 minutes are equally important.

It's very hard to pick out the great props and hookers, and put them up on some pedestal. It is not in my nature to do that because I think of us all as being the same animals, and it is unfair to pick out two or three players. It's not right to pick out Phil Kearns, for instance, because he depends on the boys on either side of him. Sean Fitzpatrick stands out, but that's because he is New Zealand captain and has had such a distinguished career.

If I had to pick out the world's greatest front row, of my time, I would go for Leonard, Fitzpatrick or Kearns, and Brown, but five minutes from now I could end up changing one or two of those names. I genuinely respect so many props, it is not an easy business to choose between them.

Front rows talk to one another more than any other

group of players on the team. We room together all the time. Before and during the World Cup in South Africa, I was rooming with Terry Kingston and Gary Halpin, and it's only natural that you feel a greater bond with them than the boys behind you or the boys in the backline. Your whole game depends on the hooker and the other prop! That's why I was upset with Brian Moore last year. We had been through a lot in New Zealand together 12 months earlier and he should have known me, and known my style of play.

I have no intention of criticising Moore just to get my own back, but the truth is that I do not rate him as highly as Graham Dawe, the England number two, who has won only one-tenth the number of caps which Brian Moore has won. Graham Dawe is a real hard man and a good rugby player. Nobody could ever accuse Moore of holding back, but the fact is that he is a little bit on the small side and he does not actually make that many hard tackles during a game.

Brian Moore is a good player, and he has made a good career for himself as England's hooker. I respect his career.

On an Irish team, I can look good one day and bad the next. That's because the team performance rises and falls far too often during the year, but it is also because of other things which people do not understand or appreciate. My role, for instance, in a short lineout is to hang around close to the outhalf, and take the ball on and set up a ruck. I'll be on Eric Elwood's shoulder and he'll pop it to me frequently during a game, but because I am seen with the ball it does not mean that I am playing particularly well.

It depends on what I do with the ball that counts. In the normal lineout, on the other hand, I am aiding and abetting and doing a few things which do not necessarily appear in any textbook, and for which I am going to receive very little praise from journalists or the public. If props did not do a blocking job, then there would be even less clean ball won in the lineout.

For the last couple of seasons, I have been at number three in the lineout but, during the World Cup in South Africa, I was at number one. A lot of people have said that I came right back to my top form during that tournament, but they did not seem to understand why? I have always preferred playing at number one, because you play a sweeping role and the position allows you to get an awful lot more ball in your hands, and run with it. And no matter what a prop does in his basic duties, if he gets plenty of ball in his hands the public perceives him as having a fantastic game.

When I started playing for Ireland I was always at number one, but then I was switched. Gary Halpin, lucky enough for me, prefers to be at number three and so he played there in South Africa. It was that simple. All of a sudden, in each game during the World Cup, I was getting the ball in my hands seven or eight times more than I had been during the Five Nations championship. I looked good in South Africa, but Gary had the harder and heavier work in the lineout, and he did the same work I had been doing for the last couple of seasons and for which I was not receiving very much thanks or praise.

Gary, whom we think of as 'Flounder', because he looks the spitting image of one of the fish in a children's comic book, knows how good I was in the World Cup and I know how good he was, and once we both know that that's all that matters.

All props do know one another. We are involved in head to head combat and with the increasing pressures in the modern game and, with increasing amounts of money now being paid out to International players, there is no question but that some individuals will resort to drugs in an effort to gain an advantage.

The front row is basically about power and technique. In the Olympic Games, shot putters and hammer throwers have to be the right size and have good timing. There is a long, long list of throwers who have been found to be using performance-enhancing drugs since athletics turned professional, and rugby union is now going to be facing the same ugly problem now that the game's amateur days have almost ended.

There is no doubt but that some people will become desperate, and will resort to any measure in an effort to gain an edge over their opponents. So far, however, I can report that I am not aware of anything happening, but unfortunately that does not mean it is not happening. Last year, some poor journalist rang me up to discuss this subject and he asked me what I thought of steroids? I told him that the nearest I ever got to steroids was haemorrhoids, and he didn't ask me too many more questions after that. But I did not mean to be smart with him. It is a bad subject, but one which rugby union will undoubtedly hear and learn a lot more about.

Naturally there have always been cases of players coming back after a Summer break, and they are a stone and a half heavier! And you think 'Jaysus! What's happened here?' And other times you notice that one or two players occasionally appear to be getting smaller!

At this stage, however, I refuse to believe that any rugby player in Ireland is taking anything. One of the advantages of Ireland having a rough time of it of late is that there is hardly the incentive for even one player to

go mad in the head and risk everything by taking a
ful of pills or sticking needles into himself.

In International rugby, there are only about two or ꞏ ꞏꞏ
players I have played against, and whom I have played
against one or two years later, who have looked vastly
different. I don't know what they did. They might have
been pumping iron morning, noon and night for all I
know, but they suddenly became twice as strong. It could
be drugs, it could be technique, or it could be hard work.

The game in Ireland has not programmed me to think
that any of my opponents might be on drugs. If I meet
someone who is as strong as a horse, I presume he lifts
weights with his teeth. That's how I think, and maybe
I'm innocent to think that way, but that's how I would
like it to be for the moment.

After playing for Leinster, Ireland and the Lions I think
I can honestly say I have never knowingly played with
anyone who has taken anything to help them in their performance. With all those teams, too, there have been no
shortage of drug tests.

Rugby is a thoroughly professional sport in some countries. In New Zealand, Australia and South Africa, players can spend two or three hours per day in the gymnasium because they have the time. In Ireland, 21 Micks in
the dressing room after a match are going to look physically different and inferior, no doubt, to a bunch of guys
from the southern hemisphere. We have jobs to go to. We
have to train, and in between we have to sit down with
our families occasionally and talk with them.

As it is, after International games, it is difficult for some
of us to meet up with our wives and girlfriends because
we have to prove to the medical world that we are not
drugged up to our eyes. I'm forever having to piss for
them.

The medical people, I know, are doing a job which is now important, but you can be there in the medical room for hours after a game trying to give them the magic 100 millilitres in a plastic jar. Once, last year, I had to provide a sample and I had 98 millilitres in the jar, and the bloke wouldn't let me go. I'd had a couple of glasses of water and three or four cans of beer by this time. I'd been into the shower, and the medical bloke had to come in with me, to watch, which was a hoot! He had to be careful that I wasn't acting suspiciously, and trying something!

In the end, I was fed up. I took a drink of water, and spat into the container. He picked me up on that, in fairness, and said 'You didn't pee into that, did you?' I said 'Prove I didn't!' I was gone after that. He should have let me out anyway, because I've done less in the past and got away with it.

But it's always me it seems! Before each match two numbers are picked at random, say numbers 1 and 17, and those two players from each side have to provide a specimen after the game. After one game against France, our hooker John McDonald spent all night in the medical room. The rest of the team had gone back to the hotel, changed, and we were sitting down to eat, and John was still trying to urinate in front of this guy back in the stadium.

The problem is, after an International match, you are totally dehydrated. You are tired and wrecked, and you could hardly spell your name for somebody not to mind, literally, pouring yourself out for somebody on request.

However, it has to be done and someday it will prove to have been worthwhile when some player is found to have had a secret concoction mixed in with his blood and water. Unfortunately, it will happen.

The price which the International rugby player must

pay is already huge. Time off work, for those of us who work, and time away from families are two major sacrifices. The International player, same as the club player, is also risking a variety of injuries, some of which he takes in his stride, and others which stop him in his stride and leave him further inconvenienced.

The backs on any rugby team are fast enough to avoid too much trouble - or at least they are supposed to be! The forwards have to look out for trouble, and that is the single greatest difference between the two of us. And then there comes the props, and we are trouble! Or we are supposed to be.

We are not that fast. We don't look neat and trim like athletes do. Most of us are not pretty, though we're not that ugly! That's being a little bit unfair.

In scrummaging, you are going to get banged and thumped a lot, and the face spends as much time in dangerous places as the boot does. It's easy to get a boot in the ear, for example, and that's what happened to me a long time ago. That's why my left side is my better side for photographers, if they cared to ask. On the right side of my head I've got a prop forward's calling card. The large cauliflower ear.

When it happened, I was in hospital for over a week. I've had more serious injuries since then. My left knee came asunder and had to be put back together again. I've had broken ribs but, really, just the usual war wounds. Nothing life threatening.

When I got the bang on my ear initially, there was a big lump of plaster of Paris hanging out of the side of my head, and I looked like a complete gobshite. The plaster was supposed to squeeze the ear back into shape. It was huge. I've had a hundred more knocks on the ear since. People are always looking at it. Kids shout 'Mammy,

Mammy! What's wrong with that man's ear?' It was embarrassing at the beginning, but now it doesn't bother me. I always have my hair cut very short. There is no point in hiding it.

I used to get it lanced after games. The team doctor would do it, and he would put a pressure bandage on it for the evening. But it wasn't easy chatting up women in the bar with a turban around my head! I don't bother any more. The ear gets painful at times, and when it becomes infected it's bloody awful painful, and I've promised myself that when I've finished playing I'll get a job done on it. Treat myself to a little spot of plastic surgery, I think. With all my millions from playing rugby!

Until I collect all the money, and while I'm still fiddling and looking around in the front row, there's not much point attempting to redesign my head. I see enough people every Saturday who, if I let them, would do that job for me for free.

CHAPTER 3

CITY GENT

I wake at 4.30 a.m., in Harrow, in north-west suburban London. I drive to the local tube station, wait for a few minutes for a train, and take the Main Line to Euston. There I wait for a few minutes for another train and take the Northern Line to London Bridge. I emerge from the depths of the city, cross the road and sit down at my desk in the stockbroking firm of Garban Europe. It is then 6.20 a.m.

This is where my rugby career has taken me to, this is my life now, a city gent! It is a far cry from tumbling out of bed in Bray at about 8.30 a.m., downing breakfast, and driving the five minutes to the Argus Furniture store on Castle Street where I worked before moving over to London.

Twelve months ago, in the Autumn of 1994, I started working in London and since it was also the Autumn of my rugby career an awful lot of people whom I like and trust thought I was mad in the head making the big jump. I was 30 years-old. And, in Ireland, it is true, my rugby career had seen healthier days.

If I had remained in Ireland, I would now be thinking very seriously about retiring from the representative game, and I would continue going through the motions with Greystones for, oh, what, probably another three or four years I suspect.

London, for me, has been a whole different ball game! Here, I have been playing for Wasps at the top of the Courage league and practically every game, every week-end virtually, has demanded the very best from me as a rugby player. Now, it is also natural for me to want to continue playing for Ireland until I am 33 or 34 years-old.

When your life is thrown onto its head, you do see things from a totally different perspective. The offices in which I work are literally on London Bridge. The Thames flows by outside our windows. St. Paul's Cathedral, Blackfriars Bridge and the Tower of London are each around the corner or just up the road. It's a change from Bray where the main view was of a Superquinn store.

I'm not saying that I have made it. By no means! But, in rugby terms, my appetite was quickly restored once I made the move, and while I am not earning huge money at this moment in my new career, the incentive is great. I can make a whole, new and interesting career for myself off the pitch. I don't want to fail. I'm working hard and learning more and more about the amazing business of brokering by the week.

The flip side of my life at present, while I remain in London, is that there is no question of relaxation. It's go, go, go. In the Winter, at the height of the rugby season, it is dark when I leave home in Harrow for work, and when I get home it's dark. Winter and Summer I must spend several hours of every day studying subterranean life in

London. The tube stations are brightly-lit and decoratively postered with advertisements for new shows and movies in the city. They are also mostly grotty. The people who stand on the platforms, and who sit and stand in the trains, all behave like automatons. Everybody stares and nobody smiles. That includes me.

It is surprisingly natural not to want to talk to a perfect stranger at 4.30 in the morning. Three of my brothers, Simon, Richard and Newton, have been living in London for several years and their lives have a settled appearance about them. My life in London has been like that of a blue-arsed fly.

I work five days a week, and then there is a match for Wasps on Saturdays. Regularly, I fly back to Dublin on a Saturday night and train with the Irish squad on Sunday morning or in the afternoon. It's back to London on Sunday evening. Up on Monday morning at 4.30 a.m., to the tube station, and so on and on.

But, I'm not complaining. It has been great. And, as I have said, I have rugby to thank for getting me here. I've also got my wife, Rachel to thank for coming over with me and giving up her career in the Ulster Bank.

I have Greystones rugby club, and a great many people in that great club to thank. Nine rewarding and very satisfying years of my life were spent at Dr. Hickey Park, and while we did not win everything we wanted to win we made the most of our throw of the dice in my time there. There were many things I would have loved to win with Greystones. A Leinster Senior Cup, for starters, and an All-Ireland League title!

It was not to be, though on the representative level I did achieve practically everything I wanted, and more than I had ever dreamed of when I first came to Greystones in 1985. I played for Leinster and Ireland, and the call-up for the Lions in 1993 and my subsequent selection for the three test matches against New Zealand was more than I had ever bargained for.

At the time, I felt that was it and, two years ago, if I had been offered a contract to go to rugby league I would have signed it on the spot. I would have done it for the crisp feel of a six-figure cheque and for the freshness of the challenge. No problem! Several Irish players in recent years have been approached by league teams to switch codes and have declined. They did not need a professional rugby career in place of their own career outside of rugby.

Rugby with Ireland was becoming humdrum. The hassle was increasing and there was no sign of the team lifting itself up above the mediocre. We were losing too many matches. Other teams around us were winning matches and in addition they were talking about earning some decent money for themselves from the game. There was no talk about greater financial rewards in Ireland. Everybody who spoke up about the Irish rugby team appeared only to have a bad word to say.

All sorts of crap was being thrown, in particular, at the team management and also at two or three of the more talented players on the team. Noel Murphy was getting a dreadful time. So too was Neil Francis. Nobody turned on me, I have to say, but the way some commentators were shooting down team members it was only a matter of time before they got around to picking me off in their sights and after me possibly, Simon Geoghegan. It appeared as though they were turning rugby into a blood sport.

On the field, as we did our very best in very limiting conditions in which to prepare, it began to feel as though the media, which included former Irish coaches and former players, were on a big-game safari hunt. Franno, with his height and by his very nature, was going to be the most obvious target. Giraffes are easy.

To see Noel Murphy, or Noisy to friends and everybody else, made out to be a bit of a buffoon was very wrong. Anybody who knew what was happening in Irish rugby and what the team and the management had to contend with, would have realised that Noisy was doing a fantastic job. He came into the manager's job at a time when the Irish players were on the point of revolt, but Noisy was like a father to us from the word go. He won us over.

He also helped the team enormously. He had a terrible job to do, and was asked to do it in his spare time, when in fact the national team manager really should be a full-time person. Noisy was getting 30 or 40 phone calls per day, and he was putting three or four days per week into the job, and for what? What was he going to ever get out of it at his age? The Irish rugby team has always lost five or six games out of every 10 played.

People looking on, in full-time commentating positions, were seriously trying to blame Noisy for those five and six defeats! It was amazing, and very wrong. The problems in Irish rugby could not possibly be the fault of one man, the same as one man, even Jack Charlton dressed as a rugby coach, was not going to instantly cure the game in this country.

Me? I needed to get away for a while from the game in this country, I suppose, and view it from afar. London has been far enough, and I can see that Ireland can have a bright and far healthier future as a rugby nation if the I.R.F.U. allows it! The Irish team needs its own identity, its own space and own time, and the Irish team and its management has to be modelled on a professional football team. Pick out any of the southern hemisphere teams, or any football team in any other professional sport, and you'll know what I mean.

I am not trying to dictate to the I.R.F.U. and neither am I making a great personal demand. Rugby has been very good to me, and from the very first day I played for Ireland, I was fully aware of the ground rules.

The first day I played for Ireland, I felt blessed just to have that green shirt in my hands in the dressing room. That's all I wanted, and I would never have dreamed of asking for a few bob or a brown envelope on the side. But, in the last six years I have put so much time into the game and I have watched virtually everybody else in the Irish dressing room sacrifice their families and their working lives without ever having to be asked twice.

Sadly, rugby at International level no longer has a place for the player who is just thankful to be receiving his country's jersey six or seven times each year. The game is now all about professionally-minded players, ambitious players, and well-funded players.

The Irish rugby player now has to think big, and prepare himself in a big way. It is the only way we can survive as a legitimate International rugby team.

I know players who have gone to South Africa for a season and they have pulled back £30,000. The same sort of money for a top player from the home countries is probably available in Australia and New Zealand. Now that Rupert Murdoch has bought up the television rights to the southern hemisphere game and is going to pump hundreds of millions into the games in those countries the leading Aussie and Springbok players will hardly be able to afford to visit us in the future! Good for them, but hopefully the game will still be in the hands of the unions.

I think rugby players deserve everything they can get.

When you observe what Francois Pienaar and his South African players did for the game and their country last Summer during the five weeks of the World Cup it leaves you without any doubt whatsoever about their standing as professional sportsmen and the size of the rewards now facing them. They did more in a little over one month than a government with brains to burn and a suitcase full of money could have achieved in a whole year.

Athletes of every shape and size are selfish creatures, and that is forgivable because time is running out on every one of us. We all face a large ticking clock. We all have only so much time and, with money now coming into the game, players want to start receiving whatever they are due tomorrow, rather than next week. They do not care that rugby has been an amateur game for a million years.

In the last ten years about one dozen strong, young Welshmen turned their backs on the valleys and the video tapes of Barry John and Gareth Edwards and the boys, and travelled up to the north of England to play rugby league. Money has always beaten loyalty in straight sets, no real contest, though most of those Welsh players went to the league game for buttons. Sums of £200,000 sound huge, but that was broken down into a signing-on fee of £30,000 or £40,000, and after that the player had to be fit and able to play X number of games for the first team over three or four years before he had a hefty six-figure sum in the bank.

There were exceptions, like Jonathan Davies, who became a hero and a rich man up north in England but most of his compatriots who were pulled away from rugby union had to work bloody hard to carve out decent professional careers for themselves. Some of them jumped about ten years too early. In the next few years, union is going to match league step for step. Union might even outrun its first cousin.

In Ireland, in the near future, some of our best players are going to see England, or possibly even the southern hemisphere, as the place to play the game. Though nobody seems to realise that, as yet, at official level.

In the southern hemisphere, they are going to be looking for top class players from countries like Ireland. The French pair, Thierry Lacroix and Olivier Roumat joined Natal after the World Cup, and the South African province also signed up Italian captain and prop Massimo Cuttitta I believe. There's the future for you already in action! The English rugby football union are placing restrictions on the numbers of players coming into the country, but Simon Geoghegan, Jim Staples, Jonathan Bell and Conor O'Shea are, I feel, in the right place to further their rugby careers and improve upon them. And I am sure more Irish players will find themselves over here.

There is a world of difference between the two countries. In Ireland, if you are playing International rugby you are probably a liability to your employer, but in England you are seen as an asset. You are also playing, week in and week out, in games which are twice as fast and hard as anything in Ireland. And that is a help to any rugby player.

England has been an enormous help to me over the last twelve months. Leaving Greystones, and leaving my old employer, John Rochford who was so very good to me, was a difficult personal decision to make, but it was the right one.

I know how I got to play for Wasps and I know how I got my job in the City of London. It was because I am an Irish rugby player. It was because of the green shirt on my back, and I am under no illusions about that. Being an Irish rugby player has given me a push down the path I wanted to take in life. Don't worry, I know I have the game to thank, though I also know that the game owed me something for the last six years. The game owes every player in the end.

CHAPTER 4

A BOY CALLED TANK

The name is Popplewell, and it's not a name which takes up many pages in the telephone book, not unless you're trying to make a call in Yorkshire. Actually, in the Dublin telephone directory, there were four of us the last time I looked. There was a Nigel Popplewell who played cricket for Yorkshire, and there is a Judge Popplewell over in the south of England somewhere. My father was two years-old when his family moved over to Dublin from Yorkshire. His name is Newton Popplewell.

Fortunately enough, I was the second boy in our family and I avoided having that mouthful for a name. That honour fell to my older brother by twelve months, Newton Popplewell ll. Naw, I'm kidding, he's Newton Popplewell just! They called me Nicholas. Nicholas Popplewell! Which is a big name, and I suppose that's why a lot of people call me Poppy. I call myself Nick Pop usually.

That's that out of the way! I was not born to be a prop forward and as a child I never thought I was big, or wide across the shoulders or anything like that. I always felt I was a normal sized kid. When I left secondary school I was 14 and a half stones, and since I was five feet and 10 inches tall I suppose at that stage it looked like there was only one place for me on the rugby field. But it's not as if my personal calling was to be a prop.

It was probably a bit of laziness, if anything, because I had been a wing forward for a long while at school. The first time I played in the front row, to be honest, I loved it. The direct confrontation, you against me, the shit or bust element to the front row appealed to me, and I am very happy that I did not end up anywhere else on the rugby field.

I was the biggest of the four boys in our family. There was Newton, myself, and the twins, Simon and Richard who are two years younger than me. Fifteen years after the twins were born my mother, Olive brought the total number of men in the family to six, counting the auld fella, when David arrived.

Until I was nine years-old, we were Dubliners, and after that we became farmers and after that we became something else. We were raised in a three-bedroomed semi-detached house in Blackrock - Frascati Park to be exact - and we were reasonably well off I guess. The auld fella had a dyeing business, and the 'e' in that is important! Because we actually sold that business and bought a farm down in Wexford. We later sold the farm and things toughened up for us all for a while.

My mother and father were to later split up, and Mum now lives in Dublin, in Cabinteely. Dad is still down in Wexford where he now has a small bakery in the town. Looking back, little David was the only boy left in the family house at the time and it was the right thing for my folks to do. It was important for the old dear to do her own thing. That's almost ten years ago now.

As four brothers, we fought like hell, which is a healthy start in life! We also fought on behalf of each other. Newton, on the rugby field, had much more natural talent than I ever had but he could never really be bothered taking the game seriously. We were on the same teams through school, which was St. Andrew's initially, later Brook House and then, when the family was living in Wexford, the four of us went to Newtown in Waterford.

Newtown is a co-ed boarding school. It was formerly a Quaker school but it was really all religions and that's where most Prods went, either to Newtown or King's Hospital in Dublin.

Chris Pim, who plays with Wesley and Leinster, was in my class down there and he was a Quaker. My grandmother was a Quaker too, so that's why we probably ended up in Newtown rather than King's. On Sunday mornings everybody went their separate ways, and I ended up going to Mass most Sundays rather than to Service in the Church of Ireland. Mass was a two minutes walk and it began at 7.30 a.m. Service was two hours later, but it meant a 20 minutes walk, and it went on for well over the hour. Mass was half an hour.

Mass it was! We popped over the wall to the Church. Or we popped over the wall and had a cigarette, and back to school! Religion was never a big topic in our household. When we sold the farm in Cahore we moved to an old rectory in Ballyoughter ten miles away, and there was a Catholic Church beside us. Some of the time the family went there on Sunday mornings. The auld fella and the old dear didn't mind, as long as we went somewhere. At Christmas time we always went to the

Church as a family, and that was great. I have good memories of those visits.

I still quite enjoy going to Church, but I would never go out of my way to get to one, I have to admit. It's mainly weddings and funerals these days, and Christmas time! Apart from that, the odd time I might have a quiet prayer. I certainly believe in God. When I'm away on tour with the Irish team or somebody else there are always a few boys who go to Church. I'm hit and miss. It's pure laziness on my part, that's all.

Back on the pitch, after four or five years as a wing forward, it was prop forward or referee, for me! I was running out of choices. I was big and strong, even though I had never been into doing weights. In school nobody ever suggested I start lifting them. I developed physically at my own pace, which can be a good thing, and which I firmly believe is better than having groups of teenagers on weight programmes. You see that in some schools in Ireland and the kids end up burning themselves out by the time they are 17 or 18 years-old.

In recent years, I have done a couple of months of weights now and again, but I have never been crackers about doing them, not like some people. I find them boring. At 18 years of age I was playing in the Gorey first team and that was a good start for me. I was introduced to a man's world and while I met a few strange, tough characters on their way down the rugby ladder it did me no harm whatsoever. I think I grew up very quickly in Gorey and I loved my two years with the club. They were a huge help to me and, after Greystones, it will always be my club.

It's hard to explain how I actually came to be the size I am, which is 18 stones, plus or minus a few pounds, but I think it was a mixture of activities, just one of which was rugby. After moving up to Greystones, I rowed competitively during the Summer months with Bray rowing club for a few years. And that was fantastic exercise. Noel Welsh got me involved. In the sea, in four-man skiffs, which are bloody big wooden boats, you would be murdering yourself. We'd be out at 6.30 or 7.0 o'clock in the morning maybe and we would row for 40 or 50 minutes. And we might do the same in the evening as well. Absolute murder.

Things like that have an effect on your body when you do them for a couple of years. In addition to the rugby and the rowing, we also did a lot of horseriding in our earlier years. My father was Master with the Wexford Hounds, and everybody in the family had a horse at one time and we all went hunting. It was great fun and good exercise.

Though riding a horse is not as difficult as rowing a boat, and while I never won very much competing on the high seas, it was not for the want of trying. Every Saturday and Sunday morning there was usually a regatta, in Wicklow town, Dun Laoghaire, Bray, Ringsend, wherever. The boats weighed a tonne. They'd crucify you! Physically they toughed me up, but mentally too you were always at war with yourself, shouting at yourself, begging yourself to give in, ordering yourself to go on. I take all my hats off to single oarsmen. They are the most dedicated and hardened sportsmen in the world.

Because of that background, I never thought of looking up a gym at the beginning of any Summer. Doing nothing else but standing on one spot and sweating for two or three months never seemed to be a good idea to me. A couple of days off and on was about it, but no record-breaking stuff.

I know I probably should be doing more weights than

I am doing, and at my age they would be useful in keeping my body in tone as I wave goodbye to the 30 mark. Instead, I'm thinking that I'll take up playing hockey again in the next few years to keep myself in good shape after my rugby career begins to come to an end. In school, I had played a fair bit of hockey too.

My last game of hockey was back in 1982, on the Irish Schools team which drew 1-1 with England. We just lost out on goal difference to England at the top of the Home International Schools championship that year, after hammering Wales and Scotland. When it came down to a choice between rugby and hockey, there was no choice.

As a hockey player, I was always stuck in the backs, and I assume the selection committee thought I would be hard to get around! I had been on the Munster team that year and we beat Leinster for the first time, so three of us qualified for the Irish side. I was never a skilful player. All I really did was stop the ball with my stick and hit it, but I was reasonably effective. It's a hard game. It's not a sissy game at all, and if you got a belt of the ball or of a stick you knew all about it. But I never thought twice about giving it up.

The family had been into all sorts of sports. My auld fella had played on the wing for Wanderers, and he had also been into horses and yachting. My old dear was keen enough too, and she had no mean left peg when it came to us kicking a ball around down on the farm.

We had 500 acres in Cahore, with beef on it, which wasn't bad. I wish we had it now! It was a good healthy life for four boys, and even though we were away at boarding school we always did our little bits and pieces when we were home on holidays. I might be guilty of over-reminiscing here, and this might sound very odd for someone who has begun a new career as a stockbroker in London, but I would have liked the farming life.

Milking and stacking bales of hay, and driving tractors about the place and stuff, it's a good and healthy life! It was unfortunate that the farm did not work out for my father, but there came a time when you could not give cattle away. It was gone! We were all sad. We had to also pull in our lifestyle considerably even though we still owned a caravan park in Courtown, the Tara Cove Caravan Park. The park has also since been sold.

At one time, we had seven or eight horse boxes around the place. I was five years old when I was sent to Iris Kellett's for lessons, and we were hunting a few years after that. The hunt was always a great family occasion. My horse was a huge beast, called The Barrel.

The odd time the saddle would roll off her because the girth was not big enough. She was the size of a barn. But The Barrel was so fat and so friendly she could hardly move. I was never going to come to any harm on her. You'd have to drag her around the place, to the shop or wherever, but it was brilliant! I continued riding until I started playing rugby seriously with Gorey.

A great many people object to hunts nowadays, and more people stand up and condemn it now than back then. I don't know, I was at 50 or 60 hunts and I'd say we might have caught two foxes. Some people will say that is two too many, and maybe they are right. As a kid you are not conscious that you are hunting down a tiny animal and killing it if you get it. As a kid you don't think beyond the moment. And the hunt was such a great occasion in a small town. Everybody enjoyed themselves and local charities usually made a fair few bob.

Drag hunting, where a scent is placed around a given course, is fairer than chasing a poor oul' fox with horses and hounds, and that should now be obvious to everybody, but people do a lot of cruel things and hunting is just one of them.

My mother and father, I guess, just grew apart over the years. I can remember arguments in the house as a kid, but in all families there are rows and arguments. Business-wise, the auld fella went through a rough time, and in the end my mother just called it a day and went back to Dublin with my kid brother. David was six years-old at the time.

It has worked out well, because Mum has built a good life for herself in Dublin and the auld fella is getting on fine down below. Their parting was amicable enough, and David also spends time in Wexford. Christmas is spent together, and there is very little friction or animosity present any more within the family. Not that my parents relationship had any effect on us as kids! Our childhood was brilliant, and we were spoilt rotten. It was a man's house, however, and I know the old dear would have liked a daughter at some stage, somebody who was there for her all the time. I was living in Dublin five years before the separation and even from my point of view it was a relief that it finally happened, because I was aware that things were not going well between them. It was tough on Mum, deciding to leave, because all her friends were in Wexford. For a long time I hoped that she would meet somebody else and settle down again, but she had no interest whatsoever as far as I could tell.

The first couple of years after the break were upsetting for us all, and I can remember the first Christmas we had. It was terrible. I was the only one of the older boys who went home. I picked Mum and David up in Dublin and we drove down to Wexford. Looking back I can have a good laugh at it all, but that Christmas was long and silent. The turkey had long conversations with itself.

I love both of my parents. There was never a time when we took sides in their disputes. The auld fella can be a tough cookie at times, but then so can I. He was always solid and fair as a father, and I was always being slagged that I was his favourite. I don't know whether it was like that or not.

He was good to all my brothers, but I do recall from the very beginning that he always called me Tank.

When Ireland play in Lansdowne Road my mother and father are there. They sit together, with David in between! Rachel is there too in case a second referee is needed, but she never is. They enjoy the games and the auld fella rushes home at the end so that he can get a last pint before closing time down in his local, Jim Frenches in Gorey. The old dear and David wait for me back in the Irish team hotel with Rachel and we have a drink together.

As my three other brothers live in London, they are more interested in going to the away games in the Five Nations. It's a tight squeeze looking after them if the three of them want to go to the one match because for away matches the Irish players only receive three stand tickets each.

For home matches, there is no great problem, or there shouldn't be, though when it comes to tickets there is no end to the problems if you are not careful! For Lansdowne Road, we get six stand tickets, and an option to buy four more, and we can also buy as many as 20 terrace tickets if we wish. Everybody takes all the tickets they can get their hands on of course and that's where the problems begin.

For a start, no player can ever get enough stand tickets.

There is always somebody who would take your arm off for a ticket if you asked them did they want one? When I first came onto the Irish scene I was a right eejit, saying 'Sure!' to every Tom, Dick and Paddy who asked me if there was 'Any chance?' An awful lot of people out there assume that the players get their tickets for free, and if he is not careful a player can end up losing the match and losing a few quid.

At this stage I have no problem telling people straight up what the story is with tickets, either I haven't got any or I have one but it costs whatever! We do not have to pay the I.R.F.U. in advance for the tickets, which is something I suppose but, because of that, younger players can feel awkward taking money off their friends. They imagine that they do not sound convincing when they say the tickets are not for free! They imagine that the other person is thinking they are trying to screw some money out of the match.

Tickets can end up being a pain in the arse, and that is a pain no player needs during the week of an International match. Now, when I get my tickets on the Sunday before a match, I try to get rid of them within 24 hours. By the Wednesday evening I want them all gone for sure. Leaving tickets in envelopes on the Saturday morning of the game is a maddening and distracting exercise, but it's a job which one or two players always end up doing at the last minute.

It's good, I know, to be able to throw a handful of International rugby tickets around the place like confetti. When that day arrives, at least you know that you have made something of yourself. For me, it was a landmark occasion in my life, playing for Ireland! Looking back on my childhood I spent so much time playing different sports that it was important that one of them could serve me as an adult, and help me.

Academically, I was average. I was doing so many things outside of the classroom that it's a wonder that I wasn't atrocious! It seems to me that if you are good at sports in school you are pulled in that direction. If your exams do not go so well, then you get a bollocking in your report, but the kid who is good at sport is never going to be locked up in the classroom.

I never had time to do much extra study. I never had time to do much detention, because that was on Wednesdays and Saturdays, and I was usually playing a hockey match on the Wednesday afternoon and a rugby match on the Saturday. With rugby, hockey, cricket and athletics it was hard for me to ever bury my head in the schoolbooks. And nobody ever buried my head for me.

At this stage, I have no regrets. School and rugby blended into one and it worked out well enough in the end for me. I now look at my little brother David, who is a clever kid, and who wants to be out playing rugby or cricket every day of the week.

Someday soon, I'm going to have a word in his ear. I'm not going to act the big brother with the heavy arm around his shoulder, but I would like to ask him a few questions. Like, what are you doing? Know what you're doing? The only thing is, if I was asked those questions 15 or 16 years ago, I'd have said 'You know what! I've got to run! Got a game!'

CHAPTER 5

THE COAST ROAD

Dessie Fitzgerald, Roly Meates and Ginger McLoughlin are three men who taught me an awful lot about being a prop forward. Dessie and Ginger gave me quick, painful lessons, and Roly took me to his home on a countless number of occasions and for hours we watched video recordings of games and talked, and with his wife Heather acting as an official, we often ended up physically re-creating scrummaging positions in the middle of their sitting-room floor.

There are lots of other people, on the tips of my fingers, whom I have to thank for guiding me and nudging me in the direction of the Irish team, though nobody more so than Roly. The man is a genius, and because he is out of the national picture right now he is a great loss to Irish rugby.

I initially didn't thank Dessie Fitz for showing me what to do. We first met back at the beginning of the 1984/85 season and I was a 20 years-old who had just moved from Gorey to Greystones and I was bursting with impatience. At last, I was playing Leinster senior rugby.

The first match I had played for Greystones was with their 2nds against St. Mary's. We won well. The next week I was straight into the first fifteen and we were playing Lansdowne in a league match at Lansdowne Road. I walked onto the pitch a man to be reckoned with and, 80 minutes later, I left the field a boy. Dessie Fitz sent me back three or four years in time that afternoon.

The Dessie Fitz I had met was a Dessie Fitz who was strong and fit, and who had just tasted International rugby for the first time against England and Scotland the previous Spring. He ate me alive, but after the game he introduced me to a friend of his, Roly Meates.

They both gave me their time and respect and, since I was just a bull-headed country boy, there was no real need for them to go out of their way on my behalf. But they did, and at this stage of my career I am now only too happy to give my time and attention to young players I happen to bump into, and try to half-kill!

Ginger McLoughlin had no real need to notice me, but he did. It wasn't during a match that we crossed paths, but before a match between Shannon and Greystones, a friendly match on a bitterly cold afternoon. It was Tony Ward's first outing for Greystones. A lot of people had turned up in Limerick and there was a right bunch of photographers and journalists milling about.

Ginger and I met and spoke for the first time, as we were both having a piss before the game. Ginger looked at me. And I didn't look back at him. I had a dose of scrum-pox, which of course is highly contagious and everybody knows you're not supposed to play while you have it. I was keeping my chin down and hoping that

Ginger did not see the mess on my face, but of course he saw it a mile off.

I had decided that nothing was going to stop me playing in Wardie's first game for us. All the people and the press who were going to be there! Too big a chance to miss. But, there the two of us were pissing away, and Ginger says to me after a couple of seconds, 'I see you've got scrum-pox.' What could I say?

I looked over at him. I presumed he was going to inform on me in his dressing room, tell everybody that there was a runt in the jacks with the pox! The referee would be told, and I would be ticked off and told to go and get back into my clothes. 'I don't give two fucks,' said Ginger as he buttoned up and turned around, 'I'll give it back to you with interest!'

I became good friends with McLoughlin after that match and he was the sort of bloke who was 100% supportive off the field. Every time we played after that he would always come up to me and we'd have good fun together, but on the field, the day of Wardie's first match, he was a hard bastard. Shannon won the game without too much difficulty.

The important thing, for me, was that I was not stopped from running onto the field at the start of the game, and did I run! Right up at the front, side by side with Wardie, thinking about how the two of us would look together in all the Sunday morning newspapers!

That was almost five years before I played my first game for Ireland. I was playing with Greystones and I was happy enough with how things were going. Greystones was a happy club.

I count myself fortunate that I ended up there and spent nine years with so many good people. It was all totally by accident that I arrived in Greystones to begin with because in my final year at Newtown School I had absolutely no idea what I was going to do with myself or where I was going to go?

With the months quickly running out, I decided to do Marketing. It was the most general thing I could think of. Why not? I got three honours in my Leaving Certificate, which surprised me for the amount of time I invested in my studies. I mean I was happily surprised. Next thing I was in digs in Carlow town and doing a Diploma in Marketing at the Regional College there.

I joined Gorey in 1982. It was my local club as a boy and they had a bloody good side there at the time. My brother Newton also played for them. John O'Doherty was one of the strong customers on the team and he took me under his wing for the couple of years I was down there. We won the South-East league twice, and there was no shortage of tough matches. In junior rugby, the one thing you are guaranteed every Saturday is at least one surprise. The players come in all shapes and sizes, and you also get some very good players easing their way towards retirement. Not that they were beyond looking after themselves!

We played against Ned Byrne, Willie Duggan and Ronan Kearney at different times. We came across some great players, and we came across lots of stray boots and fists from players who were some of the worst rugby players God ever created. There is a lot more chance of something happening and somebody getting hurt in the junior leagues because the game is invariably on the poorer side and the refereeing is often on the sloppier side as well.

When the time came to leave Gorey, I did so with lots of regrets, because everybody in the club had been so encouraging and supportive to me. Mick Weafer, Eric

Willoughboy and Jim French, for instance, were some of the boys from Gorey who regularly travelled up to Greystones to watch. Jim and Paddy Casey are two more men I owe a great deal to, and there are others though I'm not going to try to name them all here. Gorey are a super club. The day I said my goodbyes in the club was a mixture of sadness and excitement, however, because I could not wait to bang down the front door to Leinster senior rugby and shout 'I'M HERE BOYS!'

I was itching to move up to Dublin and play anywhere. Chris Pim had already started with Wesley the year before me and that made me even more desperate. I was still in college in Carlow, and I was thinking of all the years I had spent in classrooms and lecture halls. I had worked hard in Carlow and I was doing well, but I kept returning to the conclusion that I had sweet fanny adams to show for all the time I was spending with my books. I never returned for my third year which, in retrospect, was foolish.

But I felt I had made a bit of a name for myself with Gorey and, after being on the Leinster junior team, a couple of senior clubs soon got in touch with me. St. Mary's spoke with me, and Greystones, and the attraction of either club and a job was too much. Whoever got me the job first had me!

The short journey up the coast road took no time. Gorey to Greystones. Why I could have done it in my sleep, though I would have missed the beautiful scenery which comes with the journey.

Roger Boyd, from Gorey, played with Greystones for the first six or seven years while I was there, but the first person I had a good chat with was Sonny Kenny who played in the second row for 'Stones (I am now godfather to his son Daniel). Gorey has an annual festival, and Sonny was at it and he told me to come on up and have a look around Greystones. See did I like it?

It was Greystones for me, and I started my first job at Lough Egish Co-op, on Raglan Road in Dublin under the watchful eye of the late Colm Costello. I remained there for the next five years. I eventually gave up the job in 1987 in order to spend a season playing in Australia. When I came back, I joined John Rochford at Argus Furniture.

The great thing about Greystones was the speed with which the club was moving. They were only elevated to the senior ranks in 1975, and there was always so much enthusiasm and genuine effort being put into the running of the club and its teams by large groups of people. The only big thing wrong with Greystones, during my time there, was that because the club was going at such a pace the organisation was never the best! There was no central policy for recruiting senior players, for instance, and very often it was left to the 'Stones players themselves to encourage and chat up boys who might be on the move.

Competing against the big Dublin clubs, with long and hefty traditions, Greystones needed to be razor sharp with its recruitment drives, and that was seldom the case.

Nine years with Greystones was a long time, but it went quickly, especially the early years. My first three or four years there were an education and it was a bit like taking a degree course in rugby. Joe Boyle was the club's tight head prop at the time and he kept me on the straight and narrow. He also took me into his house where I lived for two years until he got married and turfed me out. I owed Joe a helluva lot. Though I also needed a little extra tuition and that is where Roly Meates came in and opened my eyes about my own ability, and just about every single aspect of prop forward play.

There was no great reason why he should have given me his time and energy like he did. Roly was with Trinity and Leinster at that time but, for me, he was a godsend. He fine-tuned every single portion of my game. He was knowledgeable and generous.

I can never say enough about Roly Meates. There were times when I was down, even later on in my career when I was struggling to get onto the Leinster team or when I was dumped by Ireland two years running, but he kept on battling away with the different parts of my game which needed improvement. We were always on the telephone to one another. It was very often technical stuff and so we would usually agree to meet up in his home.

Roly has one of the biggest television sets in the world, and we would sit down in front of this huge screen and talk and eat, watching myself and my opponents, rewinding a certain play a dozen times and meticulously picking over it in slow motion. Hours and entire evenings were devoted to just my game.

I knew by then the role he had played in the creation of Dessie Fitz, and it was easy for me to understand how Dessie Fitz had lacerated me in that first game I played against him. He had me all over the place. I was like a rag doll being thrown around. How could I, a raw young fella from Gorey with big ideas, have had any chance against the combined power and wisdom of Dessie Fitz and Roly Meates! It's a wonder I was not turned off the game for life that same afternoon.

If I remember correctly I tried to get in a cheap shot at Dessie early on, which was a bad idea. Then when things quickly became very serious between us, I tried to take him on, man to man, which was also not the brightest thing for a big kid to do. That was a good Lansdowne pack back then. There was no messing and no fooling around by their opponents.

All his life, Roly Meates has been a players' man though he is also 100% committed to rugby. God knows how many decades he spent with Trinity, and how many young players he personally accepted as pupils of the game?

It's a crying shame that Roly and the I.R.F.U. had a falling out a few years ago. The ins-and-outs of what happened are unknown to me, only the rough details. But I do know that having Roly on the outside and looking in at the Irish game is a shocking waste. Roly has always placed the team and the players first. He has always been very fortright and progressive in his thinking.

The hope is that he will someday soon return to a central role in Irish rugby. For me, luckily, Roly is still there! He's like one of those golf gurus, my own David Leadbetter! We regularly talk and if I am going through a rough time with any portion of my scrummaging game then I will not think twice about picking up the telephone to him. Scrummaging is mostly about basic positions and it's important to get the legs right, the shoulders and the arse and the neck. If you are getting one thing wrong, then your entire game can suffer. It can take a knowledgeable man to spot the exact problem, and a genius like Roly to put it right.

Whatever happens in the next few years, Greystones will always be my first love as a rugby club. Because of the distance of Hickey Park from Dublin and the virtual rural setting of the club, there is a huge sense of identity, which makes Greystones unlike any of the Dublin clubs.

When I joined, the strength in the first team had always been in the backs. John Robbie had been there before emigrating to South Africa, and they had Tony Doyle, Paul McNaughton, Johnny Murphy, Jerome O'Brien, a fantastic backline really. Unfortunately, up front, the club was never the strongest in its early years in senior ranks.

John 'Spud' Murphy and myself came into the picture in the mid-80s. Pierce Power and Joe Boyle were around, and Tom Morley was at No.8, and Tom was a rollicking good player! Howard Kiely! Suddenly, Greystones had real forward power. Brian Rigney later joined us, and Des Rigney! The pack was getting bigger and stronger, but the backs were not getting better. After having one of the best backlines in the country, and playing fantastic free-flowing rugby for two or three years, it was going to be hard for Greystones to maintain that sort of quality play.

It's a great pity that the backline of the early '80s and the pack of the late '80s never had the opportunity of spending some time together, because if they had Greystones would have definitely won everything right across the board and become the number one side in Leinster, and possibly the number one side in the country.

The record books show that Greystones, despite all the great entertainment they gave to crowds all over Ireland, have never won anything big. No leagues or cups which is a shame, but the record books which list the players from the club who played for Ireland also explain why that was. As it happened, in 1989, I was the first Greystones forward to be handed a green jersey.

Way back, Maurice Mortell, Eddie Collican and Niall Bailey played for Ireland but, having begun their careers with 'Stones, they had to move on before getting the International call-up. Five more backs made it after that onto the Irish team, before me. McNaughton played in 1978 and won 15 caps, and Robbie was capped 10 times before emigrating in 1981. Murphy played for Ireland three times, and Doyle did so twice, and then there was Wardie who joined us in 1984, having already played in 17 Internationals. He had only a handful of further appearances while a Greystones player.

It's hard to imagine that with all those great players Greystones didn't win something decent. When the All-Ireland League came into being, we were in Division Two and although we won our way up to the top flight, and did reasonably well there for a time, our squad did not have sufficient strength in depth.

But we always did well in the league against Munster clubs and that was something we were always very proud of. Greystones, as a club, was very much like a Shannon or Young Munster, and we had the same volume of support as any of them. With a hard, old pack and a great band of followers organised by John O'Neill who founded the supporters club we never felt intimidated when travelling down south. Lots of Leinster clubs do because, unlike Greystones in my opinion, they don't possess a real earthy feel for the game.

We would travel down to Munster in cars, buses and trains, and our record against the best of Munster shows that we usually ended up enjoying our evenings down there and the long journey back home to Wicklow.

The arrival of Tony Ward obviously was an enormous boost to Greystones at an important time in its history. When he came, the club had less than 10 years of senior rugby under its belt and, while some of us thought before then that Tony Ward fancied himself in a big way, he soon knocked that idea out of our heads. He was one of the best clubmen we had. On the Irish front, he had been through a difficult time, first with Ollie Campbell and later Paul Dean separating him from the No.10 jersey. But there was never any question of Wardie feeling sorry for himself.

He was a magician on the field. He should have won a half century of caps in my opinion, but Wardie was not one to bend to The Great Irish Rugby Plan, if there ever was a plan. Coming to Greystones was not a move which was going to warm too many of the game's administrators towards him. Greystones were not one of the Superpowers in Irish rugby, not on the field, and definitely not in the committee room.

A Greystones player was always going to have to try that much harder if he was to get his well deserved opportunity on Leinster and Ireland teams. The club has only been around in senior rugby a wet week in the eyes of some notable individuals in the Irish game.

The classic example of a great Greystones player being ignored and mistreated is John Murphy, Spud! He was capped for Ireland once, against Australia in 1992, but for years he was the best hooker in the country. I make no apologies to anybody for saying that, and at the same time I make no apologies for putting it down on record that Spud is my best friend.

We were inseparable for years. When I bought a house in Richmond Park in Bray he and Alan Keyes moved in, and we had a good few years together before I married Rachel and we had to throw Spud out. He was a local boy, whereas I was a blow-in and with so few players from other parts joining Greystones, and with the club being big into the community and vice-a-versa you might have thought it would have taken some time to settle in. Not a bit of it. Mick Kearney was the same as me. He joined from Lansdowne and he was a super player, but it was always difficult to entice more players to cross the Shankill Road.

Talent-wise, Spud Murphy was unbelievable. I have never known a player, at club or International level, who wanted to play the game as much as he did, and who wanted so badly to run with the ball and who wanted to tackle and tackle all day long. When we were in Australia together in 1987, Spud was 16 and a half stones and he would run for miles. His mother and father, Flo and Joe, ran two or three marathons every year. It was in his blood. He played a hard game, drank as hard as anybody and he always trained on the Monday!

John Murphy came into the Irish squad a week before the game against Australia in 1992. We lost. It was a terrible match, and he never played for Ireland again. In and out, just like that. Totally daft.

He hadn't been in the pecking order at all that season, but he got a call from Ciaran Fitzgerald on the morning of a league game between Greystones and Old Wesley, and he was told not to play that afternoon. We were all in his mother's house when he got that 'phone call. I don't know who was happier, him or me? But we told him he had to play for 'Stones, that he was probably only on the Irish bench. He was hardly in the team.

They were not going to throw him in, like that! But after the Greystones match Fitzy came up to me and told me that my other half was in the team. Nobody played well against Australia in '92, and coming twelve months after the unforgettable World Cup quarter-final match at Lansdowne Road, when we almost had them, there was a sense of a lost opportunity about the '92 game long before kick-off. Nobody on the team was up for it. We were all wishy-washy, apart from Spud of course.

He tried everything he knew and ran himself into the ground, but one man against fifteen men, who also happened to be world champions, was not exactly a fair contest, even for Spud.

In the week before the game, he had taken dozens of telephone calls every day from friends and journalists and busybodies. He had to learn a million lineout calls. He had to sleep and eat, and he had to go to work. Then, on the Saturday afternoon, he was being asked to run out onto Lansdowne Road in front of 50,000 people for the first time and play against the world champions as though he had been an Irish player all his life.

That first game is never easy, but Spud's first game was especially difficult. How can any man be assessed on just one game for his country? And when Ireland, in the middle of a losing streak, are playing the world champions how can it be right to decide that one player has not got what it takes.

It's ridiculous, but lots of players suffered the same fate before Spud. I was almost one of them myself. Twice, in 1989 and 1990, I was thrown into the dump truck after one game. The first time I was discarded after being viewed for just 18 and a half minutes. It does not make sense, but when you have large selection committees sitting down to choose teams, instead of one man and an assistant for instance, then you are going to get inconsistencies and totally nonsensical decisions made on players.

At the end of his career, Spud has one Irish cap and that is one Irish cap more than 99% of the rugby players in this country. It's proper that he won that one cap at least. People talk about 'one cap wonders' and try to feel sorry for those players, but why be sympathetic? The man played for Ireland. Spud played for Ireland, and that's something.

Nowadays the player receives his Irish cap at the dinner for the two teams the evening of the match, which is better than the way I received mine back in 1989. It was two or three months later, in fact, well into 1990 at a Leinster squad session when somebody, I can't remember who, handed me a brown envelope. Inside was the cap. I was told 'We'll get the lads together in a few minutes and give you the cap.' I said 'Don't bother!'

I took it and threw it into the back of my car. After being shafted from the team after that first game against the All Blacks, I wasn't going to do a jig in delight at being handed a bit of cloth to cover my head. It took me a while longer, a couple of years I suppose, before I realised that an Irish cap was not a bad thing to have in the house.

CHAPTER 6

MATES, SHEILAS AND PRAWNS

Another three minutes and Sunday, October 20, 1991, would probably have been the greatest day in the history of Irish rugby. Ireland 18, Australia 15. Three minutes· more. Us playing the All Blacks at Lansdowne Road the following Sunday in the semi-final of the World Cup.

Thanks a lot to Michael Lynagh the final score was Ireland 18, Australia 19. One minute, we were heroes. The next minute we were a heroic bunch of losers, and there is a mighty big difference between the two!

The saddest man in the Irish dressing room when we trooped back in after wishing the Aussies well for the rest of tournament was poor Gordon Hamilton. His fantastic try in the 75th minute, when he beat no lesser creature than David Campese to the line, should have been Ireland's most famous try ever. We all felt like death as Ciaran Fitzgerald did his bit to lift our chins up, but Fitzy wasn't to know at that moment that Australia's late victory had left his career as Irish coach virtually doomed.

It was not Fitzy's fault that the team was unable to lift itself for the next 12 months. Lynagh's try had been a final kick in the teeth for his team and, after playing some marvellous rugby that year, and receiving only knocks and setbacks and disappointments, it was as though everybody conceded that there was no question of good luck coming Ireland's way.

The team had worked bloody hard in 1991. There were no wins, only five defeats and one draw before the start of the World Cup, but we were convinced we were about to turn the corner very soon. And we would have turned that corner in some style if we had defeated Lynagh, Campo, Willie O and all of Australia in the quarter-final of the World Cup.

No such luck. No luck whatsoever. Gordon Hamilton, who had been on top of the world in Lansdowne Road that Sunday afternoon in October, barely saw a green jersey again after that. There's luck for you! A back injury soon sent him packing from the Irish squad after just one full season.

That's how Ireland's try-scoring hero against Australia was destined to end up. The rest of us had to stick with it.

Twice in four years, in Sydney and Dublin, Australia had beaten Ireland in the quarter-finals of the World Cup. Back in 1987 the result had been far more conclusive with the Aussies winning, with all the time in the world, 33-15. I was at that game. Me, Spud Murphy and Ben McAuley, three amigos from Greystones.

At the beginning of the Summer, the three of us had joined the Souths club in Brisbane. We gave up our jobs at home and headed off for six months with the intention of improving our individual games and vastly improving our social lives. And we did. We had a great time.

Ben, who played in the second row, and I were certain that we were doing the right thing by giving up work and taking off for Australia.

The two of us didn't think that Spud was going to come

along. He was hot and cold about the notion, but the morning Ben and I headed out the door to book our flights Spud decided that he wanted to go as well. We laughed at him the whole way into Dublin. We didn't think he would put his money down, but he did and it was Spud who stayed put down there for almost two years.

The original idea was to stay out there from May until the early Autumn. To show we were young and naive we never asked anybody at the Souths club for money back on our tickets. We sorted everything out ourselves. If things did not work out, we had the idea that we would scoot around the country and do our own thing. But we were soon having a ball.

Paul O'Connor from Lansdowne was playing with Souths as well in 1987. That's how the trip came about. We actually heard Wardie telling O'Connor after a match that this club were looking for someone for their second row. Of course, we were immediately all over Wardie like schoolchildren, telling him that we wanted to go too. Like eejits we never thought that they might pay for us to go over, or put a roof over our heads.

All Summer long, we worked for the Brisbane Council, me, Spud and Ben, building a wall. The Great Wall of Australia it was.

After a couple of months, because I was so good at building this wall, I was made boss over the other two lads. We had about one mile gone and there was another two miles to go. It was just a wall by the side of a busy road. Hot, dusty work it was too and a pain in the hole at times, but we were getting 150 quid a week. Because I was the gaffer, I had to be at the wall a few minutes earlier in the mornings and I had to be the last one to leave.

Not that that mattered too much to me. We shared the

same car out there and the two boys had to be in the backseat by the time I was in behind the wheel in the morning.

Souths had the entire Queensland front row of Tommy Lawton, Robbie Lawton and Dan Crowley, but that didn't worry me and Spud too much because the three of them were playing with the State most of the time. That's the way it is over there. It was Queensland first, Souths second, and whenever the three big boys were around the club then Spud and myself were thrown to one side.

It's a good system. We got loads of matches, though I had to play tight head most of the time. It was a tough few months but it came to a quick conclusion for me when I broke a couple of ribs and had to go home. That was no harm, as Phil Orr had just retired from representative rugby and I wanted to get home to sniff out his Leinster jersey anyhow. Greystones, by then, were also getting a little bit edgy because it was into September and there was no sign of the three of us coming back.

As a learning experience, it was an important Summer. In Ireland, in the last four or five years training methods have vastly improved but in Australia, even back then in '87, there was hardly any trundling about during sessions and there was total use of the ball. Everything in Brisbane was done faster than anything we had done in Greystones. It was fantastic. There was only one problem.

One of the coaches we had over us was a total lunatic and for some reason he hated the sight of me. Nobody else in the club ran anywhere for no good reason, only me! I ran for miles. And nobody knew why.

It never dawned on this stupid coach that I was not designed for running long distances. There was nothing I could do but hide behind every second tree I found, though if he caught sight of my arse peeking out he would then give me a vicious time. I can't remember his name. I just know he was a bastard.

Him apart, the Australians were fairly smart people and their club fixtures over there were based on an ingenious system. Teams play each other three times during the season, at home and away, and at a neutral ground like Ballymore. And when one club plays another the whole club goes! If there are five adult teams in the club then all five teams play against the other club in their ground, like Greystones playing five or six games against Wanderers at Dr. Hickey Park. The first game might start at 10 o'clock in the morning and it goes right through the day until the firsts take the field. It works great. Everyone in the club has a day out, watching the rugby, eating, drinking. It's a perfect system almost.

When the three boys from Greystones arrived in Australia at their own expense on a Wednesday afternoon, we discovered that we were picked for the 3rds the following Sunday. That was fine. We played well. The game was over around midday, just as it was beginning to get savagely hot. At that point, in this clever Australian way of things, I discovered that some of the 3rds sub for the 2nds. And some fucking eejit on the 2nds trips over himself shortly after half-time and I'm called into the game.

I was ready to be airlifted off the field at the end of the game. But the 2nds sub for the firsts and somebody whom I didn't know, but who was obviously in charge, asked me to make up the numbers. I thought it wise to give him the impression that there was no better man! Another dope sprains an ankle late in the game and I'm told to go in for the last 20 minutes. Please don't expect me to tell you who won what game that afternoon. All I know is that after the third game I was clinically dead. Good system, huh?

Actually, it is, and it saves both clubs on expenses. The crowd at the ground is practically trebled and, in the carnival atmosphere, rugby can appear the greatest game known to man.

Normally we played our matches on a Sunday. We worked Monday to Friday on the wall, from 6.0 a.m. to about 3.0 p.m., and after that it was far too hot. We'd go home, watch Neighbours, take it easy and get ready for training for 7.0 that evening. On Friday nights, we didn't train and instead we drove into town and tried our best to get paralytic. The general idea was to fill the table with beer and hide away enough money to someday get a taxi home.

Out there, I had no sense of direction. We had bought this great, old car, a huge lump of a thing which we got for £300. It was a four-litre tank. One morning, after a particularly outrageous night out, I had to go into town to find this car. It took me a couple of hours to locate the heap of rust, so I jumped in and set sail, but after travelling 40 miles outside the Brisbane city limits it dawned on me in my wretched state, that I was heading in the general direction of Greystones.

Spud and Ben were outside our rented mansion when I arrived back in the car that afternoon with a taxi leading the way. Cost me a small fortune. Saturdays, you see, were important days for us. We had to get mentally tuned up for the game the next day, and what we did was we would go down to one of the beaches on the Gold Coast, buy a few kilos of big prawns which are sold on the side of the road on the way down, grab a few litres of Coke, and we would eat and sleep on the beach all day long.

It was a good life. We had no money at the end of any week, but we covered the rent and we learned how to play rugby all over again. When Ireland played Tonga in Brisbane, in their third game of the '87 tournament, the three of us were there with this mate of ours. Ireland won the match 32-9, though we weren't keeping the score at any time. We were on this hill behind one of the goals called Bundy Hill. I think it's called after the Bundy Coke which is on sale in that part of the ground. A can contains a mixture of coke and Bundenburg rum, which is rotten stuff, but absolutely lethal.

We had a big bed sheet with HELLO MUM written on it and we were downing the Bundy, and looking at Ireland going over for tries all over the place it appeared to us! There was this television cameraman in front of us. We were shouting at him to wheel around and take a look at the four of us. In the end we offered him 30 dollars to beam us home to Ireland, and he must have got fed up of us because in the end he obliged. It was a pity he did because our mate had called in sick to work and his boss saw him at the game. He got the heave ho from his job. Gone. HELLO MUM and goodbye.

We were on Bundy Hill when Wales beat England and when New Zealand beat Wales. Throughout the tournament, I must confess, we were putting bets on and hoping that some of the Irish lads might get slightly injured, nothing serious, but just enough to leave them out for a few weeks. At one stage, the Welsh had called up a young prop, David Young who was playing with one of the clubs in Australia. He won his first cap in the process, and we had visions of an I.R.F.U. committee meeting deciding to save the fare on sending an Irish player all the way out and demanding; that somebody should find Spud or Poppy instead. There was no harm in hoping for a slight hamstring twinge. Irish hookers were falling like flies that Summer but Spud didn't get a 'phone call.

That first World Cup was a bit of a non-event for Ireland, although in the second-half against Australia, there was a considerable amount of spirit and guts on display. Jimmy Davidson succeeded Mick Doyle as national coach for the start of the following season, and after winning everything with Ulster for several years there was a lot of talk about a whole new Irish team.

At that time, I was having trouble gaining a foothold in the Leinster team. Orr was gone but there were plenty of boys who had been waiting for his 'funeral' and who had big ideas of filling his shoes. I was just one of them. The next two years were hard, but by the time Spud came back from Australia I had more or less wrestled the Leinster loose head spot away from the other contenders. At the end of 1989, the All Blacks were coming into town.

I was fairly sure of getting at least one shot at them, with Leinster. Tom Clancy and Paco Fitzgerald had been involved in a tug o war over Orr's old Irish jersey since his retirement and both had done very well in the Irish scrum at different times. It was hard for me to get into the picture. That's the way it was. There was a picture and if you were not in it, you were not in it! During Ireland's tour of Canada and the U.S. a few months earlier, I took the loose head spot from Clancy.

A game against a team like the All Blacks was always going to be a heaven-sent chance to be viewed, and get into that damn picture for good.

Leinster lost 36-9 to the All Blacks, but our resistance won us a decent amount of praise. Five of their seven tries came in the last quarter of the game, which was a pity but better five in the last quarter than five in the first quarter. Brian Smith, the former Australian scrum-half who had played against Ireland in the World Cup in 1987, had found himself an Irish grandmother someplace down in Wexford (in my part of the world, though I'd never met the woman!) and he had become an adopted Irishman.

There was a lot of attention given to Smith. He was a handy player, but he was nothing fantastic and it was a bit hard for other players to take seeing him handed Leinster and Irish jerseys on the spot. The papers were full of him. He was going to play his first match for Ireland against the All Blacks at Lansdowne Road. But so too was I.

Alex Wyllie's team had won something like 42 straight games at that stage. Losing to them didn't seem too bad, though Jimmy Davidson was having some difficulty building Ireland into the stronger, faster, leaner team he had repeatedly promised. Ireland were losing too many games, that was the problem. The coach was talking about the future while his team was glued to the present.

Jimmy D and I did not have much to do with one another. One game. I was discarded before the championship. Paco was back on the team, Dessie Fitz was being switched over and back in the front row, and Gary Halpin appeared in the picture. I was out again. Leinster and Ireland B was my lot. I was also looking forward to the coming of Ciaran Fitzgerald as Irish coach.

Fitzy's first game was against Argentina at Lansdowne Road at the end of 1990, and there I was, back! I played reasonably well, but we had to rely on Mick Kiernan to kick a penalty goal about half an hour into injury time to secure a 20-18 win. I was gone again. Out! Most of the pack was shafted. The following Spring there was yet another whole new beginning for Ireland, and it did not include me.

There was a new captain for the championship, Rob Saunders, who was full of beans even though he was just out of nappies. Simon Geoghegan and Jim Staples were introduced, and the front row was Paco, Steve Smith and Dessie Fitz. Ireland lost to France, drew with Wales, gave England a bloody hard time of it before letting them win the Triple Crown with a late try, and in the last game in Edinburgh Ireland lost to Scotland, 28-25 in a thriller.

The results could not have been much worse, but the performances were excellent. Ireland played a bold, open style of rugby and looked to be going places.

The only place the team went that Summer, however, was Namibia, and once there the team went to the dogs. But at least I was on the 'plane, and there was a chance of squeezing myself back into the frame of things. Namibia was probably the last place Ireland should have gone in the middle of the Summer in preparation for the World Cup a few months later.

We had a 21 hours journey to Windhoek, including a five hours wait in Johannesburg in the early morning, and when we arrived we headed out to train within an hour of touching down. It was hot and sticky. The ground was bone hard. And there were bugs, of the unseen kind, ready and waiting to delve into this big bunch of white Micks.

There was very little which was good about that tour, apart from the fact that I ousted Paco from the team. We lost both test matches against the Namibians who had only won their Independence 12 months earlier. They were too fast and far too clever for us, but then their entire party did not have stomach rot! We looked like a sick team and played like a sick team, but people at home hearing the results didn't care to know that the Irish team

Going for a walk with my big brother Newton, along Dun Laoghaire pier. I wanted the umbrella!

A mean-looking bunch? Newton, me (with the lunches) and the twins, Simon and Richard on the first day back at school (1970 I think).

The Big Day! Richard, David and me, Dad and Mum, Newton, and Simon on my Wedding Day in 1992.

Getting some encouragement on my wedding morning from the kid brother, David, my best friend Spud Murphy, and my Best Man, Brian Rigney.

Rachel and me and a nice bunch of flowers.

A world exclusive? The claw sucking his thumb! Clohessy and myself making up our minds about beating England, at Lansdowne Road in 1993.

Who said props just push and shove? A scrum half against Wales in 1994 (top), and something of an out half in the same game (Bottom).

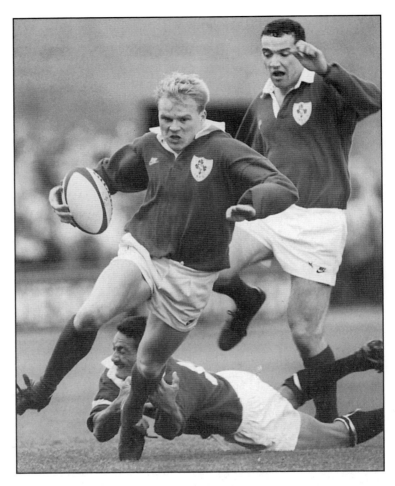

Simon Geoghegan, with Conor O'Shea offering encouragement, stretches his legs against the United States in 1994.

How a Prop should sidestep (above), and how to keep one eye on the ball and one on Kyran Bracken (below) against England at Lansdowne Road last season.

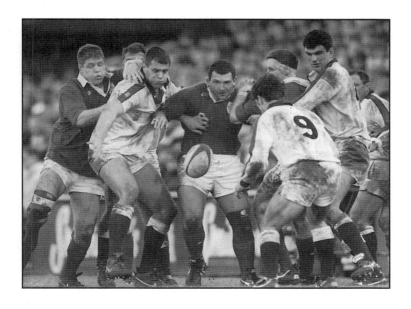

The Claw, Woody and myself in 1994 on national duty (above) and in Barbarians uniform (below) against South Africa at Lansdowne Road.

would have chosen to play both test matches in the bath-room if they could have.

The World Cup, at the end of 1991, did not hold out too much promise for Irish supporters, not when they con-sidered that the poor Namibians had failed to qualify for the tournament. We were in Pool 2 with Zimbabwe, Japan and Scotland. The winner of the group was due to play a quarter-final match at Murrayfield against Wales or Western Samoa (it was Western Samoa surprisingly). The runner-up in the group had Australia at Lansdowne Road more than likely. Zimbabwe and Japan did not pose any great problems, and I helped myself to two tries in the first game, though Brian Robinson - the greedy gut - scored four. Early in the second-half against Scotland at Murrayfield in the deciding group game we led 15-9. We were full of steam, but the Scots ripped the game from our grasp.

We left the field with a bloodied nose and we were im-mediately criticised for not sorting out the Scots. But the game, which we were controlling, had turned on its head, so fast!

Armstrong got their winning try, and sure we were an-gry with ourselves after the match. They did what they had to do and they got away with it.

A fortnight later Australia would win the World Cup, beating England at Twickenham in the final, after first taking care of the All Blacks in the semi-final, but they were the luckiest team in the world to leave Lansdowne Road alive that day against us.

We had the wind in the first-half, but for 20 minutes we were imprisoned in our own defence. Campo soon went over for a try after splitting us in two with a crazy change of direction. At that point Ireland could have decided to try and kill Campo or somebody, and try to get back into the game that way. Or we could have played good rugby.

As I've said, it was in the nature of that Irish team, all year long, to play good, attractive rugby. The team had been doing it since the first game of the Five Nations championship. We began to get our game together, and although they won a lot of lineout ball we felt we had the better of them in loose play, and they knew it too. We knew it was one of those days when we were going well. They knew they were in trouble.

Ralph Keyes kicked two penalty goals and we were level at half-time. Lynagh and Ralph brought the score to 9-each early into the second-half, but then Campese got his second try. Time to start packing for home or dig even deeper? We were already dug deep into the game. There was no decision to be made on the field. Campese's second try didn't knock a feather out of us.

Jack Clarke had a couple of chances to do damage on the left wing, but he hadn't got that little extra injection of pace which Keith Crossan had always given to Irish teams. Jack, at the third time of asking however, when Staples had hacked the ball downfield, somehow gained possession and then fed Gordon Hamilton who took about half an hour to reach the Australian line, it seemed to me. He still arrived there before Campese so he must have been going faster than I thought. Ralph hit a magnificent conversion from the left touchline. It was 18-15, and we had beaten Australia.

We had no idea how much time was left, but it was hardly very much. Everybody was dead on their feet, Irishmen and Australians, and we just knew it was just about over. There was five minutes left. From the kick-off we fell back into defence, and Rob Saunders had a chance to reach touch with a kick. The ball never got there. The

Aussies won the next scrum, and seconds later Lynagh was in for a try in the right corner.

They had the coolness to do the right thing, and to do everything right at the right time in the match. They didn't go for the dropped goal. They looked for a try, and that took something special from a team which was about to have its dream blow up on them at any second.

Afterwards, the Australians were relieved and they were almost thankful in a funny way. They knew they were blessed. They were cool and smart when they most needed to be, but they were still blessed.

There must have been nobody praying for us at the end of the game. Everybody in Ireland was either staring in disbelief or hollering. We had Australia beaten. We beat them. In my heart I will always believe that, fat good that it does me.

CHAPTER 7

DON'T CRY FOR ME, IRELAND

The whole country was pulling its hair out for three years, 1990, '91 and '92, watching the Irish rugby team. A lot of people were mad as hell with what they saw. Their mood was understandable. We didn't just lose games. We had England, France and New Zealand clocking up record scores against us practically every time we ran onto the pitch with them. Still, it could have been worse for the man on the street.

He could have been the man on the Irish rugby team! I made my championship debut right plonk in the middle of a 10 game losing sequence in the Five Nations, dating back to the end of Jimmy Davidson's reign as Irish coach, through Ciaran Fitzgerald and into Gerry Murphy's time in charge.

To be perfectly accurate, nine of those games were lost and one was drawn against Wales in Cardiff Arms Park, which had become one of the few places on this planet where an Irish rugby team felt safe and sound. What was wrong?

How could Ireland almost beat Australia in the World Cup in October, 1991 and just a few months later lose all four games in the championship? There are lots of excuses and explanations. Good reasons why we blew hot and cold, and never stayed hot for very long. But would anybody have listened to us?

In October, we were the next best thing to a team of heroes, but the following February we were being booed by our own supporters (the same people who had applauded us all afternoon against the Aussies). Everybody loved Ralph Keyes during the World Cup. They could not hand him enough awards in December and January, but in February as we lost to Scotland in a dreadful game Ralph was jeered every time he kicked the ball.

The Irish public had enough and the Irish players did not know which way to turn. We honestly didn't. There was not much fun left in playing for our country. Confidence was almost at nil. Training sessions helped to raise our spirits only briefly. There was not enough of those sessions and the work we were doing when we did get together was clearly insufficient or inferior, one or the other, maybe both.

Am I saying that we should have shot the coach? That Jimmy D should have been put against the wall first, Fitzy after him and, for good measure, Gerry Murphy?

Naw, no point! Irish rugby as a whole was to blame. The game in this country did not see, ten years ago about, that rugby union had changed from being a social game and had moved into a serious and lucrative business. To be honest Jimmy Davidson, Ciaran Fitzgerald and Gerry Murphy were not bad coaches.

I went on my first two Irish tours, to France and North America, with Jimmy Davidson and even then, back in 1988, he was way ahead of his time. Jimmy D was also a bit over the top some of the time. He needed somebody to tone him down when he was talking to the players and also when he was talking to the Irish public, because he set targets which everybody knew were not reliable, given the support which the national team was receiving from Irish rugby as a whole.

From the highest committee in the I.R.F.U. right down to the lowest of clubs, there was no agreement that the Irish team should take pride of place in the general order of things. Practically every club in the country was meeting more often and having a greater amount of time together than the Irish team.

In Ireland, the club still comes first, whereas in Australia ten years ago the club came last. Nobody was allowed to get in the way of the provincial team or the national team.

If Jimmy Davidson had the Irish team seven days a week then he might have got somewhere. We would have needed that much time because we were moving from a standstill position to meetings where cardiovascular stuff was being discussed. It all happened too fast for the players. We looked at ourselves, however, and saw that we were obviously not in great shape according to Davidson's programmes.

The Ulster boys had Jimmy D as their coach for several years and they were in better shape than the rest of us. It was also Jimmy Davidson who was the first coach to tell the players to stop reading the newspapers. His thinking was: why look for criticism and insults? He was right to a point, but at the end of the day we all know that journalists are, at worst, a necessary evil. They are doing their jobs and by not working with them you achieve nothing. You only worsen your situation in fact. It is important to play the game off the field too, whether you respect your opponent with the notebook or not.

The job of Irish coach is a tough one, however, and it is much harder than the job of any single player. I would not do it for the world, believe me, especially when Ireland is never going to win 90% of its games! That is not being defeatist. It is being honest. Ireland have never, ever, won even 50% of the games we have played.

Why be coach and be abused after losing a few games, and have your family, your children, and your friends and workmates affected?

Jimmy Davidson isolated himself by his ambitious nature and that did not help him. But he could not help himself. He was so into the whole thing! If he is to be remembered for one thing, then it was his philosophy on physical fitness. He was the first man to tell an Irish rugby team what targets they should be aiming for.

When Ciaran Fitzgerald followed Jimmy Davidson, it appeared that he could fill the void between the old coaching ideas, which were basically to turn up as fit as you can, and the new philosophies. He was a player from the '80s and he was a coach for the '90s, and he looked the right man.

I admired Fitzy greatly. I was in the Irish squad which toured Namibia and New Zealand with him, neither of which were historic trips. But Fitzy gave the job everything despite overwhelming odds. The Namibian safari was poorly planned and the whole team was ill at one point or another; whereas in New Zealand the squad was severely understrength because of the absence of half a dozen of our key players.

Fitzy is a great coach and with a stronger squad at his disposal he would be a match for any coach in the world. Fitzy did not have the players and while that is an excuse which any Irish coach could trot out, in his case it was very obvious that he was not meeting with the correct response from the team in match situations.

I know this may sound harsh, but I do not think Ireland

has ever had 15 true International players at its disposal at any one time. There has always had to be some plugging and filling in the teamsheet. It is only in more recent years that our inadequacies are being shown up. And that's because other countries, with a greater number of players to choose from and with greatly improved training programmes, are showing the difference between us to be black and white.

In the two very disappointing seasons experienced by Ciaran Fitzgerald, he always stood by his players. Even when we failed him, he never publicly turned on the Irish team. Fitzy, right to the bitter end, which was our bad defeat by Australia 12 months after the 1991 World Cup finals, never stopped trying to build us up individually and collectively. He was brilliant in the dressing room and he deserved better on the field.

Gerry Murphy and Willie Anderson filled the middle of the room after Fitzy, with Willie being the dominant figure and very similar to Fitzy in his methods of motivation. Willie belonged to the forwards. He was missed when he left in a hurry after two years.

Gerry Murphy was a good bloke and a nice guy, but he did not have the presence of Jimmy Davidson, Fitzy or Willie. It's difficult to say whether Gerry was good or bad as a national coach, because he was never on his own in the players' eyes until after Willie Anderson left the scene in 1994.

Even then, other people were helping Gerry like Noisy and Pa Whelan, and in the run-up to the World Cup in South Africa the training routine and preparation were decent enough, but it was never the best. Everybody was doing their bit, but it was obvious that we needed one man in a professional capacity in total control. Somebody the players could listen to and think about, and worry about. Somebody who would make us want to impress him simply by his being there. Pa Whelan, I would have to say, did a very good job with the forwards in a short space of time, and we had endless sessions of lineout practice, rucking and mauling. And his work showed against Wales and New Zealand in South Africa.

I was on and around the Irish team for three years before making my Five Nations debut in 1992, at Lansdowne Road, in the opening game of the championship against Wales. We lost 16-15. The whole ground seemed to be quiet and depressed by the end of the afternoon, even though there was only one point in it, and even though the fantastic World Cup game against Australia was still in everybody's system.

People expected so much that day. The 1991 championship had seen Ireland play thrilling rugby, and then we should have beaten Australia! Then, one of the worst Welsh teams anybody had ever seen, beats us. That one point defeat was like 50 points and it ruined the entire championship.

A few weeks later Willie John McBride announced to the entire country that an Irish cap had become a cheap commodity. I think that's how he put it in his newspaper column. It made me wonder what Willie John, in his prime, would have been able to make of life as an Irish rugby player in the early '90s. The world game had changed. Would Willie John have been able to show far greater consistency than say, for instance, Neil Francis?

Willie John McBride did his thing in his time, but being an Irish forward 20 years later was not all about having a big heart and raw strength. The whole game, on and off the field, was far more complicated than that.

I'm not saying Willie John McBride would have struggled in the '90s, but he would definitely have struggled to become the rugby folk hero that he was. We lost to England 38-9 at Twickenham. They scored half a dozen tries exactly. Scotland were next, and the Scots were without Finlay Calder and John Jeffrey who had both retired after the World Cup. We had them in Lansdowne Road.

We lost 18-10. Our fifth defeat to the Scots on the trot. It was during that match that Molly Malone and all her friends left Lansdowne Road and all we could hear was booing every time the ball was near Ralph Keyes. It was a sad day for Irish rugby.

The end of the season was even worse for all of us. Four weeks later we had to play France in the final game in the championship, and we had to play New Zealand in two test matches.

There was no place we could hide, not in France and New Zealand. Though we were starting to lose players thick and fast. Brennie Mullin announced his retirement. Philip Matthews, who was captain of the team during the championship, was injured and pulled out of the tour. Philip Danaher took over that role.

France scored 44 points against us, which was the highest total Ireland had ever conceded in an International match we were told afterwards. We scored 12 points. New Zealand was the greatest test ever faced by an Irish rugby team. The squad which arrived in Timaru, in the pouring rain, in May was without Geoghegan, Curtis, Mullin, Keyes, Saunders, Crossan, Dessie Fitzgerald, Francis, Lenihan, Matthews and Hamilton. They all had their reasons, good, bad and indifferent.

New Zealand was not the most attractive place on earth at that particular time, and it was awful bloody cold. The week before we arrived six Queensland players had to be treated for hypothermia after a match against Canterbury and the referee actually stopped the game well before the end because of the distressed state of some players on both teams.

We won our first match against South Canterbury 21-16, which was our first win since we defeated Japan in the World Cup the previous October. It didn't rain that afternoon either thankfully. In the squad there were only five players who played against Australia in the World Cup. On the tour there were eight matches, and in truth all eight were entirely forgettable by the time we came home.

Okay, we came within a nose of becoming the first Irish team to beat the All Blacks when we only lost 24-21 in the first test in Dunedin, but our performance was one of pure desperation and actual terror. We were scared stiff of being beaten by 90 or 100 points, as some of the provincial teams had put figures in the 50s and 60s up against us. The whole tour was a complete and total mockery.

After that first test, some of the boys ended up in tears in the dressing room. Granted we also put a huge amount of pride and spirit in that one performance, but I kept my tears for a game further on down the road in Cardiff Arms Park!

Twenty-one points was Ireland's highest score against the All Blacks, and that was something. Vinny Cunningham and Jim Staples both scored tries in the first few minutes and we were 12-0 in front before the All Blacks had finished their Haka practically. We showed great guts for the rest of the game alright and in the scrum we were well able for them on the day. They scored two tries. Cunningham got a second. They got their third. It was 18-each at half-time, and it was some game I suppose!

But we lost! We made all the running and they still caught us, and in the second test they ran all over us. We were gone early on in the game. Our legs were gone and we had not got the heart for another torrid battle. I just wanted to get home. All the boys did.

There, who did we have waiting for us the following November, but Australia! That's France, the All Blacks twice, and Australia we had played in-a-row. The Australian game was another bad, depressing afternoon and I'm sure they must have hated that match as much as we did. It was a non-event. Like it never happened, though Fitzy announced his early retirement as coach the following week.

Waiting around the corner was the 1993 championship, and defeats by France and Scotland. That brought Ireland's dismal run into the double figures. The team had soaked up so many disappointments and insults and, we didn't know it, but we were about to burst. With anger, hurt, and so many other things. They say an animal is at its most dangerous when it is wounded. So what were we?

If there was one place we were going to do something about our suffering and humiliation, it was Cardiff Arms Park. Bread of Heaven, indeed.

Ireland had not lost in the Arms Park since 1983, and at last we had something to play for. There was a proud record to upkeep. We were able to forget about our hard times. If we lost, there was no place left to go. It felt that dramatic.

My crying after the game was something which caused me no embarrassment. I was called Ireland's Gazza, and I didn't mind getting the mickey taken but myself and Gazza cried for different reasons and that should not be forgotten. He had lost a game. We had won. And, in fairness, there were a lot more people than me in tears. I was the one who happened to ask the cameraman for a handkerchief, that's all. I'm only a reasonably emotional person. But the years of losing, the torment of the bad press and the hurt which grows, were so great that I don't think any of us fully realised it until Sandy MacNeill from Australia blew that magnificent whistle.

For once, we weren't the worst in the world. A victory, 19-14, peace and prosperity! Eric Elwood had played like a veteran in his first championship game. Pat O'Hara played like a giant. Denis McBride was a small giant. Mick Bradley was the best scrum half in the world. I don't mind saying we were all powerful - me included!

Brian Robinson scored our try in the first-half and Eric kept us there with his boot for the rest of the game. Ciaran Clarke had kicked a fantastic dropped goal to get the performance rolling. MacNeill gave them roughly, I'd say, a million penalties in the second-half. Ieuan Evans scored a try after a pass which was two miles forward. You win some, lose some.

The game we won! I had played 17 times for Ireland and at last I had won a game in the championship. Could you blame me for getting sort of watery?

Soon as the post-match dinner was over, I left the hotel that night with a couple of the boys, and we were not going in search of drink. I needed to walk up and down the streets for a while. Watch the Irish supporters, and really believe that we had come good.

After our very next game, in Dublin, a happy taxi driver refused to take his fare from Rachel and myself in the early hours of the morning. Told us he had been paid enough having watched Ireland that afternoon. Would you believe it!

CHAPTER 8

RIDING THE CHARIOT:
AT LANSDOWNE AND TWICKERS!

The Wednesday night session before an International is always reasonably violent. But the Wednesday night before we played England at Lansdowne Road in 1993, in the last game of the championship, was something else. Somebody could have been murdered.

Everybody, I suppose, was still very emotional and excited after beating the Welsh in Cardiff. Though the Wednesday is always our last, hard scrummaging session, and after finishing off a day's work and rushing around a bit to get to the team hotel, and then get to the training ground, most of the boys are pumped up. It's nighttime, there's floodlights, and the opposition pack usually has a few individuals who try to get cheap shots in and want to look good in front of the selectors.

In fairness, if I was down the line and was asked to make up the numbers against an Irish team, I would have no problem myself in availing of the opportunity to roughen up some of the big heads and prima donnas.

It turned out that I had to leave the field with a cut leg that Wednesday night. Nosiy (Noel Murphy) said afterwards they thought it best to take me off, before I did damage to somebody else! Peter Miller, whom I was scrummaging against, also had to leave the field with a bloodied nose, but I don't know who was to blame for that, honest! Peter and I had been on our first Irish tour together, to France in 1988. He did not get the same breaks in his career as I did, but he was a good, honest player and he was always tremendously fit.

I was wired-up, I must admit. I was extremely nervous, thinking of England, and thinking about the Lions and who might be selected. Ken Reid was Ireland's representative on the selection committee and Ken was giving me a running commentary all the time. Every time we would bump into one another he'd say something, like 'You're just in at number two spot at the moment.' Ken and I get along very well, and he was trying to be helpful.

The next morning England were coming into town, but when you're playing England you're as ready for them on the Wednesday night as you will ever be. There is a natural in-built animosity in the Irish nature when it comes to meeting England on the playing field. They are the old enemy. And they are so bloody good! You know that if you are not totally on top of your game you will get hammered.

You are always afraid. You think back to the times they have stuffed us by 30 points or whatever, and all the times we have had to walk off the field after those ridiculous defeats.

On the Friday night before the game, some of us had to go down to Searsons on Baggott Street for a few pints. Earlier that afternoon I was in bits. Seriously! There were a few of us highly nervous and we knew with the way we were feeling that a few pints were going to do no harm. We were back in the Berkeley Court shortly after 10 o'clock. And I slept like a baby!

To beat England, we knew we had to go as close to breaking the laws of the game as we possibly could. That was the very least we had to do in order to avoid another hammering because, at the beginning of the day and at the end of the day, England are a far better team than Ireland on paper. Therefore, we have to just not be offside. We have to hold them down as much as they will hold us down in the lineout. We know that every single, last man has to spoil his opponent at every opportunity.

England needed a good win to clinch the championship. France were playing Wales the same afternoon, and France were eight points ahead of England in the table. The championship was being awarded on points difference for the first time, but all of that was of no importance to us. We just wanted to beat the stuffing out of England. Stop them doing the same thing to us!

I was up against Jeff Probyn, and on the previous afternoon at the A game between the two countries, which England won, we had almost bumped into one another. The two teams were sitting together at the game, which was not a good idea.

Probyn is a good boy and a good friend (and we were to later play together at Wasps). He also had a good game that day against us and he was bloody unlucky not to be included in the Lions squad which was named 24 hours later. If you had to pick one English forward at Lansdowne Road that day you would have picked him. He was attacking like mad. He did his usual aiding and abetting in the lineout, but it was the second time in his career he was passed up by the Lions.

After the match, at the dinner for the two teams, we

were sitting together, Probyn and I, the two of us full of drink! And Geoff Cooke, the England manager, who was also going to be managing the Lions team down to New Zealand was sitting in front of us. I'm sure Probyn knew the story with the Lions by then, but I didn't, and the two of us were there nodding and winking at Cooke, acting the fool, and giving him the thumbs up.

The two tight heads who had to be picked for the Lions were Probyn and Peter Clohessy. The Claw had a superb year. And the Lions selectors go and pick Burnell and Wright, the two Scots! It made no sense whatsoever, which was later proved during the eight and a half weeks on tour.

I had played with Probyn on the Barbarians team against the Australians earlier that season, when the two of us agreed with our direct opponents, McKenzie and Crowley, walking the field before the game that we wouldn't contest the scrums. We agreed that we would take it easy on one another, and Probs and I had great enjoyment in welching on the deal in the very first scrum!

That was four or five months earlier, but in Lansdowne Road, as both packs waited for Eric Elwood to kick off, I just knew that Probs was looking in my direction. I knew he was. I didn't want to look up at him, but at the last second I did. And he had a look on his face, a kind of grin which said 'No deals, Pop.'

Sandy McNeill, the Australian referee, was in charge and that was good. He was the ref in Cardiff two weeks earlier as well. It suited us, but if we could have picked a ref to have for the English match it would be one of the French fellas. They like to keep the whole thing flowing, and they don't believe in blowing up for every little thump and fart. They refuse to do it.

McNeill was okay though, and like a lot of refs he

knows we're a good sporting country, that we do not like getting beaten, but that we are very good losers. Which we should be, of course, because we get a lot of practice at it.

Aussie and French referees usually give both teams a little bit more leeway than normal. And that suits us, especially against a team like England. Eric kicked the ball to start off the match, but before anybody got a touch on it Paddy Johns took one of their lot completely out of it. It was a penalty to them, but it was a fantastic start for us. It's one of those things which we always say we will do, and sometimes it happens and sometimes it does not. Paddy is not Ireland's most aggressive rugby player, and for him to do that triggered the entire team. It was great. We all knew it was going to be an interesting game right from that point. We won the game 17-3.

It was eight years since Ireland had last beaten England, when Michael Kiernan's drop goal at Lansdowne Road won our last Triple Crown. That was back in 1985. It was my first year with Greystones. My first year in senior rugby, and we had played a game that morning and we watched the Ireland-England game in Jim Doyle's pub in Bray.

This time we didn't need a last-minute kick to win it. We knew we had the game won long before the end. The English boys were in on that little secret too.

The amazing and funny thing was that we won the game in the lineout more than anywhere else. On paper, that should not have been possible. They had Johnson, Bayfield and Rodber. We had Francis and a few pygmies. But on the field it was so different.

Irish teams have always been bad lineout performers, which makes it difficult nowadays as the lineout has become so important. There are so many of them as opposed to scrums. Direct penalties into touch give you the throw. It's an easy way to get into opposition territory. Or else teams are always hitting the ball parallel to the touchline, down the tramlines, and getting their opponents to kick it in. That way a team can find itself in an attacking position in five or six seconds.

Willie Anderson was in charge of the the Irish forwards, and he had 15 or 20 different combinations for the lineout. Which is good, but difficult if you are a prop, because since we're not the brightest, we can become totally confused.

On top of that, there's an awful lot of cheating in the lineout. Any International referee will tell you he could give five or six penalties at any one lineout, because somebody is swinging, somebody else is holding down, somebody is lifting, pushing, shoving. It's a lottery in which there is one winner only, and lots of losers every time.

Short lineouts are different and allow much more movement. They also offer the element of surprise. Willie had decided on lots of short lineouts against England as well. Eight of us would head towards the line, and the hooker would get the ball in his hands, and five of us might split out immediately. That was going to leave England wondering, and before they knew it the ball would be in and out (hopefully!).

I was at number three in the line, as opposed to number one which I prefer and which allows me to get more ball, and drive forward more. Galwey was at number two and Johns at number four, and I was looking after them, shunting them up, as well as disrupting the opposition. There were quite a few digs going in from both sides, I have to admit to that.

The two English props, Probyn and Leonard, were up

to their usual tricks too. They're both cute in the lineout, and they have an awful lot of experience. Their support work on the ground is second to none on either throw in.

There were some big hits being put in all around the field, and Pat O'Hara was phenomenal. He is the hardest tackler I have ever witnessed up close, but it was Elwood and McBride, together, who totally creased Rory Underwood early on and really set the agenda for the rest of the day.

Everybody was putting in tackles. We were so scared of them scoring one try, and then quickly scoring two or three more, and making fools out of us again. Claw, Terry Kingston, myself, we were all putting people down, and when you have the front five tackling all over the field you know you are going to be okay.

It is no good to any team having the back row stuck down at the bottom of every ruck. Eight forwards tackling and covering ground makes all the difference, and it is the way the modern game of rugby has to be played if a team is to have any notion of winning a game. Eric kicked a fantastic penalty from the left into the wind to put us in front, but it was 3-3 at half-time. Stuart Barnes hoisted a high ball. We had somebody taken out of it, but we also had somebody, I can't remember who, who gave an English player a slap. I don't think it was a punch or anything. The penalty decision to us was turned over to the English and Jon Webb kicked it from in front of our posts.

We had the wind in the second-half pushing us down the field, and we were soon 9-3 up. From a lineout Eric dropped a goal, and after O'Hara nearly killed Dewi Morris in one tackle, we won a penalty and Eric kicked from 40 or 50 yards out. We were playing England, and we were coasting! It was an amazing feeling.

Their hearts were no longer in the game. It was easier for them to think of the Lions trip rather than deal with a field full of totally mad Micks. I remember coming off the field and thinking that it was one of the easiest games I had ever played in in my life. It was no such thing, of course, because we were all black and blue, and fucking sore, but the minute the game finished I thought to myself that I could turn around and play another 40 minutes, no trouble.

Galwey's try at the end was the result of a dreadful pass from Carling out to Tony Underwood. Geoghegan and a couple of the others were up on Underwood, though I don't recall exactly what happened. That was one stage of play I was definitely half a mile behind. It was Mick Bradley, I believe, who finally ended up with the ball before giving it off to Mick Galwey. But it was Will Carling's fault, and normally Will never makes silly mistakes. He is a classy player. But the pressure we applied left the English team looking like a bunch of hired individuals by the end of the day.

It was like one of those cowboy movies. We were the ordinary townspeople, and they were the hired guns, but they didn't want to know about it once they found themselves in a real fight. That is one of the great faults with the English team. The team unit breaks down into individuals fairly quickly when sufficient pressure is applied. The pity is that Ireland are unable to stand up to them very often. We see them as being so much better than we are. And they are better, but that does not mean we shouldn't be able to beat them now and again. We're only talking about 80 minutes. It's not like we're being asked to play rugby against them for 80 days running.

England were without Dean Richards on the day, and any day England are without him is a day when they are vulnerable, in my opinion. He is such an important player.

Dean is also a hard man. When he is playing, England sometimes have seven or eight hard men, and when he is not playing sometimes they have none, though Tim Rodber is also the sort of player who gets other players running through stone walls with him. Rodber, in time to come, looks the natural successor to Carling as team captain.

I'm not saying that Dean Richards is the sort of player who swipes all around him. He seldom needs to resort to that. He is a deterrent rather than an instigator on the field. He's just so naturally strong and boney, and big on the field, and he has such presence during some games that he can almost set up mauls on his own. He soaks up everything the opposing team throws at him. It's no wonder he looks to have been on the field for eight or nine days at the end of nearly every game he plays.

Richards is not a rugby player who could ever be created in a science laboratory. He is the perfect specimen of a natural rugby player.

In practically every game you verbally abuse your opponents now and again. Against England, near the end of the game, I suppose we were shouting our mouths off a fair bit, especially in the scrums. I never said anything to Probyn. I would respect him far too much to start down that road with him, but I enjoyed myself with Brian Moore. 'Come on, Brian' that sort of stuff. 'Good boy, Brian… No Brian, that's no good.' Claw and myself had several good chats in the scrum. 'What you think Claw?… Will we push them back a bit?' It's okay doing that in Moore's face, because he would be the very one who would be rabbiting on and laughing at us normally.

Stirring the shit like that in the scrum is not always a

good idea, but against England that day in Lansdowne Road, we took great delight in stuffing it down the throats of one or two individuals. It's not often we have England on the rack. They were in pain, and we were dead right to smile at them.

That night was good. We can say what we like about the English, but they know how to enjoy themselves after a game and, like us, there are no better drinkers than the English. By the end of the night, it was back to normal and we were all the best of mates.

In the next couple of months on tour with the Lions, I learned so much more about the English boys. I can honestly say they are the best bunch of players I have ever been with, outside the Irish team, of course. It was mostly their tour. They had the bulk of the squad, 15 or 16 players, Geoff Cooke as manager and Dick Best as assistant-coach. Carling could nearly have been captain.

The defeat at Lansdowne Road was obviously not the deciding issue in Will not getting the Lions job. All the background work had been done long before then.

Ian McGeechan was the coach, and he and Hastings had a good working relationship which was going to be vitally important over eight and a half weeks of non-stop rugby. Gavin was the better choice in my mind. He is a better person to bring 26 players together and make them instantly feel like a real team. He did that quickly. Gavin is a very sociable person, as is Will, but Hastings is far more of a players' player. One of the boys. There was also an inkling, in addition to that, that Carling might not be able to sustain his place, and as it turned out that was the case in New Zealand.

While I got on well with the English players, I can not say the same about the English management. I can hardly recall having one single, personal conversation with

Geoff Cooke throughout the two months which followed. Not that I was bothered by that, since I was playing reasonably well and I was getting most of the Saturday matches before too long. If he did not see any need to talk to me, then so be it!

In the back of my mind, however, I wondered would we ever meet in a hotel corridor and have a decent chat. As a manager of a squad, I found him a little peculiar, I have to say. He had most of the English boys around him so he probably knew what he was doing. He certainly could not be compared to Noel Murphy on a personal level, though Cooke's track record as team boss is fantastic.

McGeechan was brilliant, a fantastic guy. You could talk to him about anything. But Dick Best was, what can I say? How can I put this? He was not the sort of coach I had ever met before, and he was not the sort of coach I ever wish to meet again.

Dick Best and I were not the best of friends, it appeared to me at the beginning of the tour, and our relationship sort of went downhill very fast from there. Which naturally did not make life very pleasant for me since he was in charge of the forwards. Mick Galwey, the only other Irish player on the tour from the very start, was not able to help when it came to working out between us what exactly Best was about.

Cooke was a sort of shy, reserved guy, and he would never be rude or act the heavy. Best, on the other hand, is renowned for his very strange sense of humour.

Best is also a Harlequins man and he coached Jason Leonard, my direct opponent for a place on the test team, for years. Naturally I quickly assumed that Best was a Leonard fan. In the last couple of weeks on tour, when Leonard had to be moved over to the tight head side because the two Scottish lads in the squad were not playing well, Dick Best became a little bit friendlier towards me. That's the way it appeared to me. But me? I told him to fuck off. He didn't seem to want my company for the first six weeks, so why should I need him?

But did he make me suffer on that tour! He had me running all around the place. We were doing an awful lot of physical sessions, and for us dirt-trackers (those of us who were not involved in the Wednesday game) there was always something special laid on by Best. He put us through hell. Five or six of us. Though, I'm not saying he was all wrong. The Lions tour went well for me, and it would be very foolish for me to say that Dick Best created any problems for me which were not surmountable. He certainly geed me up, because I could not stand the guy and now and again I would burst myself, just to show him.

Though I didn't burst myself every day. He might have me doing 50 or 60 press-ups, for some reason, and I would do 30 or 40. He might tell me to run left and I would run right. I had no interest in getting into his good books. He's a difficult individual to work out, though he had a successful reign with England, and he is very highly thought of at 'Quins. On reflection, I now know that he did get the best out of me on that trip. And, I guess, I should now say 'Thanks, Dick!'

For most of the tour, I was rooming with Dewi Morris. He was a big help to me, and any time I felt low or was worried about something he would be there to help me out. And I would help him too. In the first-half of the tour, in Wellinton, I suffered a dead leg against the Maoris and I had to leave the field. Leonard replaced me. I thought at that stage that I had blown the test team, but

Dewi supported me like somebody who had been helping me for years.

On a tour like that, you need somebody to talk with. You need lots of reassurance from time to time. In the Irish set-up, I can talk to Noisy Noel and he will iron out any problem. I wasn't going to ever approach Best. McGeechan was fine, and Hastings was always there to be of help, but the first three or four weeks were very difficult.

With Ireland there are 14 or 15 boys you can have the banter with, and you're confident that what you say will not go any further. There is a great trust. It takes a while on a Lions tour to have that same sense of unity.

The previous Summer, Ireland had been on a disastrous tour of New Zealand, when the only thing which mattered was somehow surviving to the end together without the whole team being suffocated by the humiliation of it all. With the Lions, there was the smell of success, and that made players more likely to look after themselves first.

The Lions began with one week of physical preparation. After beating North Auckland fairly impressively in the first game I got my first run against North Harbour, when I teamed up with Kenny Milne and Paul Burnell in the front row. We won again, but there was a right punch-up in the second-half and with all our forwards rowing in practically, the game helped to inject a lot of character into the squad.

It was in the third game, on a fierce wet and windy day against the Maoris that I got injured. We won 24-20, but we had been 20 points behind at half-time. It was an heroic comeback by our boys in the last 20 minutes, when Ieuan Evans, Rory Underwood and Gavin scored tries, but having to leave the field just before we redeemed ourselves did not do much for me.

The team was continually rearranged in the opening weeks, as the management looked for their best fifteen for the first test against the All Blacks at Lancaster Park in Christchurch. Myself, Milne and Burnell ended up as the front row. The Lions lost the game, 20-18, to a last minute Grant Fox penalty goal. We were unlucky. And the Australian referee Brian Kinsey didn't help us any. With two minutes remaining, we were ahead 18-17, thanks to six of the best from Gavin's right boot, but then Frank Bunce was setting up a late attack when he was tackled by Dean Richards. And Richards was winning the ball from him as the tackle turned into a ruck. Dewi Morris was shouting at Dean's heels. But Mr. Kinsey decides for some reason that Dean was holding onto the ball. That's what he told us afterwards, but why would Dean want to do that 40 yards out from his own posts?

Another funny decision from the referee, early in the game, had given New Zealand their try. Bunce was again involved. He caught a big hoisted kick from Fox on our line but Ieuan Evans was also in on the action and nobody could be sure what happened when they hit the ground.

By the time of the second test in Wellington, I had been joined in the front row by Moore and Leonard. That second test was the best and most exciting game of rugby I have ever played in in my life. Twelve months earlier Ireland had almost beaten New Zealand in the first test of our tour, and some people felt we should have won. The truth is that we were a bit of a joke out there.

With the Lions, it was all so different. In the first test we had been unlucky to be denied by that last gasp penalty goal, but if we had won that opening game then the second test would probably have been a totally different proposition, with them coming at us from every angle.

It turned out that we conceded an early try and got off to the worst possible start. Hastings spilled the ball underneath our posts which is so untypical of him. However, the knowledge that the whole series would be down the swanny if we lost, made everybody fight back right from that point. For the rest of the game we put so much pressure on the All Blacks.

I do not think I have ever played in a match where the opposition was under such pressure, and it was a magnificent feeling - against the All Blacks of all people! I was scrummaging against Olo Brown, who is a great player and a good friend of mine at this stage. I met him for the first time during the Irish tour.

Playing in the Lions pack, that day, it was like being part of a machine rather than a body of men. Leonard, it must be said, did a fantastic job coming in for that match at tight-head. We won 20-7. Easy. Peter Winterbottom was unbelievable, and he made Michael Jones look a mere mortal. Rory Underwood scored a try which came after a sizzling move and ended with John Kirwan being made to look pedestrian. The All Blacks big guns could do nothing to stop us, and their pack could not move us! Our proudest moment came midway through the second-half, when we were leading 12-7, and the All Blacks needed to do something fast to get back into it. We were defending a five yards scrum from our own try line. They HAD to score. They had options, like a back row move on the blind side, or they could have sent one of their big wings down the middle. They decided to go for the pushover. Sean Fitzpatrick struck the ball cleanly and it rested at the back of the scrum. They set themselves for the second shove, squeezed, dipped and PUSHED.

Nothing happened. We did not budge. Back to the drawing board, boys!

The All Blacks learned their lesson that afternoon, and duly used it to their advantage. The only other Lions side to win a series in New Zealand were the 1971 boys. In 1983, with Fitzy as captain, all four tests were lost. The final game this time was in Eden Park, which is the spiritual home of New Zealand rugby and where they have only ever lost once in the last 600 years or something like that. The official programme, I found out afterwards, contained a warning, 'The All Blacks win. It is as simple as that. It is the birthright of every Kiwi to presume victory.' Fancy that. They won 30-13, and they took the series.

We had been 10-0 up in no time with Scott Gibbs getting in for a lucky try. But we could have had no complaints about what followed. They played as though their lives depended upon it. We played to make a little piece of history. Gavin had a bad day and couldn't do very much right, but their back row was phenomenal, particularly Jamie Joseph. They scored two tries before halftime, and for the remainder of the game we were playing up a big hill. It was unfortunate that it ended as it did because by the end of the tour there was a great spirit and sense of camaraderie on board and it was a shame we did not emulate the achievement of the 1989 Lions who had travelled home victorious from Australia.

By the end of the tour, I had Dick Best at my feet almost! I had been appointed judge at the beginning of the tour by the players' committee, I don't why, but I think that former England prop Paul Rendall had always been judge when England went away. It must be a job handed down to loose heads! Judge Popplewell it was. We had plenty of good courtroom scenes, after all the big matches, with crates of beer from the local brewery in the middle of the floor.

The defence attorney on the trip was Stuart Barnes, and I must say he had a lot of work to do, arguing down some very strong charges and other charges which simply seemed like a good idea at the time. Snoring! Being nice to a certain journalist, those sort of criminal acts! The prosecutor was Brian Moore, and as he is in that business off the field, so anybody brought up before me was in for a tough time.

Richards and Wade Dooley were the two court enforcers, so there was no way out for the poor player or coach who had been sentenced. The Welsh players were up in front of me a lot. They are renowned for being extremely cliquish. And they are. They hang around each other all the time. It's incredible, they are brilliant guys, and they are great tourists, but if one of them heads out the door of the hotel to go to the cinema the whole lot of them have to follow him. If one goes to a particular pub they all go to that pub.

At the beginning of the tour, they received ten dollar fines each, and they were told not to be seen talking to one another for 24 hours. Later on, at one sitting of my court they were ordered to spend a night out with their wrists tied together. The whole lot of them, one big Welsh family!

The idea behind the court, in addition to having some harmless fun, is also to break down barriers between the players from different countries as quickly as possible. At one particularly highbrow function early on during the tour, I had the entire squad of players ordered to scratch their nuts four times, or incur a 50 dollar fine, every time they spoke to a female. It worked a treat I must say, and since the High Commissioner's wife or some decent woman to that effect met our party at the doorway to the reception it looked like the whole lot of us had fleas from the word go.

Who should be brought up in front of me one evening, but Dick Best! It was the night after our victory in the second test. Before the game the squad had bet on the final score, the usual thing where whoever is closest gets to keep the pool of money.

In fairness, if you were smart, and you were watching everybody else put their money on the Lions to win, as we all did, then the thing to do was to go for the All Blacks. That is what Dick Best did, God love him. But for some reason I went easy on him, and I only told him to down a bottle of champagne or something. By the end of the night, however, I thought he looked quite ill!

He had the good sense of fun to appear before the court, I must give him that. He knew he would receive no mercy from the judge!

For me, however, it was back to the coalface, and back down to the bottom of the Five Nations championship the following season. We lost to France and Wales in our first two games, and the fantastic ending to the 1993 championship when we beat Wales in Cardiff and beat England in Dublin, looked to have been a brief respite from the hounding we were getting from the media.

Everybody was saying we were no bloody good, once again! Our third championship match, in Twickenham, was only going to give England the opportunity to laugh off their defeat in Lansdowne Road twelve months earlier. That's what we were being told.

The mood within the Irish camp was far more relaxed than it had been the week before the England game a year previously. Nobody knew what to expect. We knew England wanted to beat us very badly, and we also knew that they fully expected to win handsomely. But Dean Richards was not in their side. Tim Rodber was in, but Ben Clarke dropped out through injury a couple of days before the game and Steve Ojomoh from Bath was in for his first cap. The referee, by the way, was a Frenchman, so everything was not in England's favour by any means.

We had 12 of the previous year's team playing, with Conor O'Shea coming in for Ciaran Clarke, Maurice Field in for Vinny Cunningham, and Neil Francis in for O'Hara. So we had Franno in the lineout, but we would not have O'Hara knocking down people all over the field.

Admittedly, it did not look as though England would be beaten by Ireland for the second time in succession. They had three big wins at Twickenham behind them, and that included the scalp of the All Blacks, and they had only scored 16 tries! Ireland's last win at Twickers was back in 1982. England had not lost in the ground in the championship, to anybody, since 1988.

It was all enough to make an Irish rugby player go out the night before the game and have a few quiet pints. And, naturally, that is exactly what a few of us did. We were staying in the Chelsea Harbour Hotel. A smashing place, and we found a pub to our liking around the corner. We had just sat up at the counter, when one of our number noticed some of our management team sitting across the bar from us. We had our few pints. There was no point sitting there drinking orange juice and worrying, was there?

The next day was fierce warm. It was a glorious day if you were not on your way to Twickenham to play against the tallest and strongest rugby team on our half of the planet.

The afternoon, as it happened, did not go too badly at

all. After 37 minutes, Simon Geoghegan got it into his head to score one of the greatest tries an Irish team has ever concocted. 'Swing Low Sweet Chariot' never sounded sweeter, that's if you could have heard it properly. For a team which was sure to lose, Ireland were playing well, and there were an awful lot of Irish supporters, about half a million of them, who had taken the bother to travel over to the game.

Unlike in Lansdowne Road, this time England were winning a lot of ball in the lineout, but most of their possession was scrappy and there was no sign of then throwing the ball around with any great purpose. Usually in Twickenham, against us, England score a try and everything happens from there.

With no try on the way, England began to panic and the team which had been told it would win the game handy obviously began to wonder exactly how it was going to happen. England began to break down again into individuals, and acts of desperation. Plan A had been to score lots of tries against the Irish, but England did not seem to have a second plan.

We knew they would be going for tries, and we knew they would start to get edgy once those tries had not come. Our try was brilliant. Bradley whipped the ball out to Eric and he fed Philip Danaher, who threw a beauty out to Richie Wallace, coming off the blind wing. Wallace passed to Geoghegan, and there was still a lot of work to do. Simon had to go outside Underwood, and still beat Callard for pace. A dream score, and Eric then kicked the conversion from the touchline. Brilliant.

In the first five minutes of the game the entire Irish team, practically, had said a big hello to Kyran Bracken, who had been one of the heroes of England's victory over the All Blacks a couple of months earlier. I've done some television work with Kyran in England, and I get on well with him. He's a good boy. But he is an Irishman!

We found this opportunity early on to re-route a ruck when we spotted Bracken on the ground. We forgot about the ruck and just went over Bracken instead, and it definitely did give him the opportunity of getting to know most of the Irish boys. About five minutes later, in another ruck, Peter Clohessy had a short conversation with him, just the two of them this time, about who Kyran should really be playing for.

I heard an awful lot of talk after the game about our try and where the move originated, and how it was textbook stuff. Different people were given credit for its planning, going back several years, but I haven't got a clue about where it came from. It was a great try, but without Geoghegan, textbook stuff or not, it probably would not have been finished off.

Simon has stuck his neck out often enough on his likes and dislikes about playing for Ireland. He does not get enough ball, I know that, but he's like Rory Underwood. He is fierce hungry and when the ball does reach his wing he devours it and the ground in front of him. He wants it so badly.

At half-time, I had to have a piss. It was one of nature's badly timed demands, I'm afraid, especially with Twickenham having been done up to the nines and looking like a temple to the game more than a rusty old rugby ground lost in suburban London.

It had to be done there and then, on the hallowed turf! With the sunny day and the few pints I had the night before, there was nothing I could do about it. It was no big deal really. Just got down on one knee, and hoped that all the photographers with their zoom lenses were pointed in Will Carling's direction.

The relief was considerable, even though there was not that much to do as it turned out. It must have been mostly nerves. It happens now and again, and in the middle of a game there's no point arguing with yourself and trying to convince yourself you don't have to go. It's better to do it and get on with the game. Twickers wasn't damaged at all, I can assure the English rugby union.

While I was doing that, Franno was supposedly talking to the whole team and telling them what was needed in the second-half. That's what people looking at the game told me, that Franno did most of the talking during the break, but he was probably just breathing heavily with his mouth open! Franno, seriously, did say a few things alright. It was good to hear him, because Franno is one of the best players in the world when he is on song.

England were still looking for that one golden try in the second-half, and they were winning good ball and they had a scrum on our line. Elwood put in one great tackle on de Glanville. The try did not come, however, and a Callard penalty left us just 10-9 in front before Geoghegan put us on the right road again. From defence he kicked the ball long to the English 22 metres line, and he was up to tackle Rob Andrew in possession. Andrew conceded a penalty for not releasing the ball. Eric kicked it. Another Callard kick had them back at our heels, 13-12, and there were 17 minutes remaining.

The Claw put in an amazing tackle on de Glanville, I think it was, right out on the touchline and a million miles away from any other living person. It is one of my lasting memories of a great win. The Claw does what has to be done whenever it has to be done. He fears nobody and nothing.

The English scrum was wilting a bit, by the end, and with their Triple Crown and Grand Slam hopes looking like they might be going down the swanny, the entire English team began to creak. Andrew has since told me we were cheating bastards, and that he was penalised in the wrong when Geoghegan jumped on him. Rob actually took the defeat very well, but a lot of other people were moaning about our final score.

To hell with them! Irish teams have been done over so many times in exactly those same circumstances. It happens to us all the time. And anyhow, in every single game there are a dozen incidents which tug it one way or the other. It is small-minded to pick out one moment and announce that it was decisive.

In those last 17 minutes we were getting the ball in the scrum and talking to Moore and a few of the English lads. 'What's it feel like to lose again then, Brian?' In the last seven or eight minutes we had a good few scrums and we were able to waste three or four minutes. We just kept trundling slowly forward, and talking.

The English were desperate. Their back row had fanned out most of the time, and there were still eight of us pushing them. It was an unfair contest, but it is rarely you ever have the edge on an English scrum and when you get the opportunity there is no point in not enjoying it. 'Will we go for a little nudge Claw?... Will we bother?'

There was a champagne reception for us in the Hilton Park Lane, no less, that evening. After beating England two years in succession, we deserved nothing less in my book. During the evening, I had to talk to Pat Kenny on his television show. What a chore! He kept on telling me that Simon Geoghegan had been fantastic. I kept on asking him: 'Who?'. I must have had a few drinks on me.

That night I was sitting next to Brian Moore over dinner. He was quiet. He was big into the defeat, and I didn't bother talking to him about the game at all. I decided to humour him, because it's not often you get the opportunity to humour the likes of Brian Moore and his buddies.

I was also sitting with Dewi Morris, my old pal from New Zealand, and as he had been sitting on the bench all afternoon he was not desperately sad that the team had got beaten. Will Carling came up to me, asking for some ancedotes from the Lions trip so that he could slag me off in his speech.

I said, 'Will! Anything you want!'

CHAPTER 9

GOING TO THE MOVIES

'What are you ringing me for?' asked Rob, in his office in London. 'Come on over! Let's have a chat.' On the Lions tour in the Summer of 1993 Rob Andrew and myself had become good friends. Regularly, I would call him and some of the other boys in England and talk, but that morning I 'phoned Rob he obviously guessed by our general conversation that I must have had very itchy feet.

The Lions trip had been approximately 10 months earlier. Another championship had ended. Ireland lost to France and Wales, we had beaten England at Twickers, and disappointingly drawn with Scotland in our final game. There was no stopping the Irish team on its world travels, however, and after touring New Zealand two years earlier the team was now going to head down to Australia in the Summer of 1994. However, I had decided that I would not be going.

I had just finished three years of virtual non-stop rugby. I'm talking about 36 months of go, go, go! I was tired. Totally wrecked.

But, after deciding that I would not be on the Irish plane taking off for Australia and before telephoning Rob Andrew, I was physically stopped in my tracks. The cruciate ligament in my left knee snapped. The same injury which Gazza, Alan Shearer, and a host of well known G.A.A. players have suffered in their time. Brian Rigney, the Bestman at my wedding, had come a cropper the same way three years earlier.

I had badly wanted to take a rest from the game, but there is a difference between resting and working your arse off every day in the gym in a frantic effort to get back playing rugby. Big difference. However, I had time to think about my career and it was obvious to me that if I didn't take a break from Ireland I was more than likely heading downhill. It was time to go, even if I was dragging my left leg behind me.

I needed a change of scenery, away from Greystones, but there was no way I would have considered joining another Leinster club at that time. I would also have felt guilty, I think, about joining a Munster club.

Work-wise, I also felt the need to go and do something else. John Rochford and Argus Furniture had been so good to me. And to even think of leaving them made me feel the most disloyal bastard in the world, so I ended up just doing it. I 'phoned John on the Sunday night to say I would not be in on the Monday morning. John and I had been like brothers. I had to physically stop myself from going into the store in Bray the next morning. If I had gone in that morning, I was there for life.

For somebody who has not got a degree behind him, I knew that my opportunities were always going to be few and far between. And when my best rugby days ended? It was definitely time to do something, and that's why I was calling the English boys and chatting to them. I had signed forms with Bath and London-Irish the previous year, and Rachel and myself had gone over to Stuart Barnes in Bath for a weekend, but I just did not feel right about the move at the time.

I had done my knee in right after the championship had ended, playing for Greystones against St. Mary's in the league. I had problems with the left knee all year, and I had some clean-outs done on it, but there I was against Mary's running along and BANG! It was like being shot. I've never been shot! I picked myself up off the ground. Greystones scored a try and we were receiving the ball from the kick-off, and I went to pick Riggers (Rigney) up and the whole knee went underneath me.

That night, I had a few pints in the clubhouse. I stayed around, which was wrong, but at least I did not go out dancing. Thought about it alright! The next morning when I woke up the knee was huge. Immediately I rang up the Greystones Doc, Brendan Cuddihy and he organised for me to see Brian Hurson in the Blackrock Clinic. Brian told me the worst. He's tops in the world in his field, but when I had to go into St. Michael's in Dun Laoghaire to have the corrective surgery done I was still worried that my rugby days might be all over. I had the operation on the Thursday and on the Friday I was trying to bend the knee, and the I.R.F.U. paid for everything in my time of need, fair dues to them. Brian Hurson did a brilliant piece of work, the medical care I got in Michael's was terrific from all the boys and girls, and everything worked out well thankfully.

Though it was not all that simple. I had to work myself to the bone, literally almost (well, I lost a couple of stones!) in order to get the knee right again. The worst part, after the operation, was that I could not piss. I couldn't move, and I could not do anything into the container they gave me. While I was on my back nothing was happening. Gravity was having none of it! The nurses were running taps, whistling, everything, but nothing came. I was there for a day and a half, and I was close to passing out on the bed.

In the end, standing up, with a nurse on either side of me and my arms around their shoulders, and with one of the saintly girls holding the container, I discovered peace and happiness once again.

Eleanor O'Keeffe, the physio at Greystones, played a magnificent role in getting me back to full fitness, and Riggers, bless him, had sufficient patience with me when I 'phoned him twenty times a day, for weeks, telling him the knee did this and the knee did that, and asking him what he thought? I went back to work for two weeks, but my mind was not right and the standing and moving all day was not helping my knee.

In the health club in the Royal Hotel in Bray, I did an awful lot of work in the water, running on the spot in the deep end. I was there every afternoon. Always the same spot, and I'm sure the women in the aerobics club down at the shallow end thought I was some class of strange pervert.

All the work I did was geared to getting back to playing rugby again and being in the same shape I was before the injury or hopefully even better. I also had this vision of my career ending after the World Cup in South Africa. I had to do something more with my life. It so happens that I am prone to making fast decisions, which is a good thing and a very bad thing.

So, I went to London and met Rob, Dean Ryan, and Peter Carroll from Wasps over lunch. I knew what I wanted to do. It was something I had to do, and without even taking the opportunity to discuss the whole move with

Rachel, I reached agreement with them by the time coffee was served.

It was for my own good, and it was not going to hurt Greystones that badly in the long run. I was going stale with them and there were good young players coming through onto the first team who would offer more to the team in the next few years than a tired or bored Nick Pop would. Those were the facts of the situation.

What exactly the men from Wasps thought of me during the course of that lunch, I don't know! Because I was something to look at. Some sight. I was starting work the following week as an extra on the Mel Gibson movie 'Braveheart' and the Lions prop who walked into the hotel to meet Rob and the boys had crutches and a full beard, and with all the physio work I was doing I was a lot slimmer than they imagined me.

I must have looked the image of one of Long John Silver's buddies. Still, there was a place for me to fight for in Wasps and I knew I would soon be ready to do so.

The first person in Greystones I 'phoned was John Murphy. Spud would understand. He didn't believe me at first because he knew all about the Bath business, but I told him that this time I was on my way. It was hard for the club at the time. Riggers had left two months before me, joining Shannon, and some people possibly thought that we had reached our decisions together but that was most definitely not the case. It was unfortunate and accidental that the two of us decided to leave at about the same time.

There was a night out down at the club for the pair of us, and it was a happy, quiet event. Then I went off on the piss with Spud. I felt sure that, after a little while, there would be no ill-feeling whatsoever in the club towards me. I also felt that if I stayed around and started playing like shit then my long and very enjoyable period at Greystones would end up badly.

After nine years, it had to come to an end. It was sad to have to go. People like to have International players associated with their club, whether they are playing well or not. It was sad for me too. Everything which happened for me as a rugby player happened while I was at Greystones. Leinster, Ireland B, Ireland, the Lions! But that's life.

And you only have one life, and it must be lived to the full. At that time I was sure the future for Rachel and myself lay in England. Rachel's Dad, Pat Kerr is a former president in Greystones. He played for the club, and he has held most positions on the committee. I first met Rachel when I was working temporarily in the Ulster Bank. She was into hockey, and she watched a lot of rugby, but a few years passed before we met up after a match and started going out together.

Moving to London was exciting and risky for us. I had no job and I was entering a new club. I had to look for a house for us. Rachel stayed at home and continued in her job in the bank for the first few months.

At 30 years of age I had an opportunity to start afresh, and my legs were good for another four or five years. I aimed to make the most of those years. The Last Chance Saloon? If Twentieth-Century Fox decide to make a movie of my life I will have to think up a better title than that. Though I can tell them that I will be able to play myself as an older man.

Dodgy knee or no dodgy knee, I was in the movies in 1994! Most people who live in Bray are in the movies at some time in their lives, I suppose, with Ardmore, Mary Tyler-Moore and Neil Jordan hanging around the place. A few people I knew were getting work as extras in the new Mel Gibson movie, and I had given up my old job at the time so why not?

The money was not fantastic, but the couple of months which followed were nearly always interesting. The craic was often great, and being up on a horse mostly every day was very good exercise for my left knee I was medically informed. I was also told, naturally enough, not to fall off.

The good news and the bad news was that the horse I was given for the two months closely resembled an elephant. It was a monster, and although he did not move too fast, I still felt a bit of an eejit stuck up on this thing and risking everything. If the boys in Wasps only knew where I had gone after lunch?

It was an awful long way down from the top of the horse. I had to prove to the movie people first that I was a competent rider, and when I had done that they handed me a massive, long lance. And a shield. Riding therefore required a lot of leg work and it was hard enough to balance everything at first but I got the hang of it. A couple of weeks into shooting I had learned to rest the lance on the horse's head. He didn't like it. And he probably thought about bolting on me every so often, but we had a good relationship overall and neither of us came to any harm. Or at least I didn't.

We got used to one another. I never got his name. I stuck to calling him Elephant. It was a long, old day up on Elephant because you might have to start at 5.0 a.m. and there were days when we did not finally finish up until 10.0 p.m. Seventeen hours! Or you might be up at 7.0 a.m. and finish at 7.0 p.m. which was usually the case. Obviously the man (Mel or whoever?) who was putting all the millions into the movie wanted action around the clock. I would demand the same if I was throwing in a few bob.

The movie was actually costing 50 million quid, I was told, and it tells the story of Sir William Wallace who decided to have a private war with the English after seeing what Edward I was doing to the Scots. The English fancied themselves back then, you see, and they even came up with the idea that they could bed all Scottish brides on their wedding night, whether they were married to them or not! We were either Englishmen or Scots, depending on which side of the battlefield or the camp they were shooting. Actually I was an English cavalryman and I was a Scottish nobleman, though it was a pain in the arse on a hot day being the English fella because I had a rake of stuff on and this big metal hat. I'd be dying in the heat. The Scottish thing I wore was a bit like a skirt, and if I was in need of air all I had to do was lift it up in the air and let in a good breeze.

In the last few weeks of the shoot the whole process grew tedious. People were narky, and they were ordering us all about the place. All these assistants and half-wits, and assistants to the half-wits, and all of them thinking they were some class of Spielberg. All through, at least, we usually had the best of the best to eat.

We were with Mel a lot at the beginning. He might be at the next table or something, though I never marched up to him and asked him was there anybody sitting next to him. Talking to Mr. Gibson was not allowed. Talk to him and it might be the last time you'd open your mouth! Midway through the whole thing, when there was about 150 horsemen, there were too many of us for Mel's tent, and we were all thrown out. And given our own tent to eat in.

The couple of thousand F.C.A. boys who were being

used did not have it like us, God love them. With the strain and the hurry to finish the thing, the F.C.A. boys were not being treated like a bunch of Robert de Niros. They were getting totally pissed off, I could see! We'd hear them too. It was around that time that Mel came to them personally to thank them for their good work and all this complete rubbish. It was just aimed at keeping a smile on everybody's face until the thing finished. He signed photos. Had a laugh, and after that nobody was allowed to say boo to him ever again.

Mel was alright. He knew how to have a laugh when the time was right. One time, he needed to have a piss in a hurry and he ran into this small forest. There were sheep in there, and we all started baa-baaing him, which drove some of the Spielbergs mad as hell. But Mel reappears with this big lump of old sheep's wool hanging out of his fly for us all to see. We chuckled over that, me and Mel!

I enjoyed myself most of the time. But there were so many takes that the F.C.A. boys were beginning to lose the cool a little bit and their morale was drooping. Silly things always happened, like 'Take 10! Thanks to that little BASTARD at the back with the sunglasses!' And 'Would the peasant at the back take his watch off, PLEASE!'

There were classic battle scenes. You see, we'd be really bored for a few days and then every so often we'd be told to rip into one another! And there were one or two metal swords around the place! We had not received any real lessons or anything but I reckoned we looked far more realistic than the actors did up close, because we just went berserk.

The lances were made of pipes and stuff, and the swords were metal, wood and plastic. Chances are you'd have a wooden one and you'd run into someone with a metal one, but everybody had metal hats on and occasionally when the battle scene had ended we'd go up to a foot soldier and clatter him over the top of the head. His helmet would be squeezed down over his eyes and his ears would be ringing for a few minutes. Served them right.

I got quite a few clatters myself, but thankfully I never fell off elephant. It was important not to try to snooze when I was up on elephant. There were chancers walking around the place loosening girths and you'd find yourself in a heap in the middle of a scene in a second if you did not keep your eyes opened.

Elephant and I were together right to the bitter end. For him it was bitter. He was having a fling with this other horse. She was in a different field and elephant tried to jump a ditch to get to her. He landed on his back. He was grand afterwards, but it was nearly the end of him.

At the end of 'Braveheart' I instantly decided that I was retiring from the movies. In September of 1994 I was on my way to London, and it was only six months since I did my knee in but I was fairly fit and I was feeling strong.

My next role was to be far more interesting and testing than my last. I had to be a Wasp.

CHAPTER 10

INTO AFRICA: WORLD CUP DIARY 1995

WEDNESDAY, MAY 17:

Tomorrow we finally arrive in South Africa! This is it. What we've all been waiting for, and what an awful lot of people at home in Ireland seem to be fearing. Are we heading for our greatest humiliation with the whole world watching? I don't know. Nobody can know. All we can do is our best. But I can tell you that I'm not going out in order to make a complete fool of myself. And I don't fear anybody either! To hell with them. And to hell with the All Blacks first of all.

This morning we flew to London, where we had to put our bums down on seats at a Guinness function for a few hours. All to do with sponsorship. All to do with big business and money. And yet a lot of people say rugby players should not hold their hands out for as much as a penny. The way the game is going something is not adding up!

Anyhow the Guinness thing was alright. There must

have been 400 people there, and I met a couple of old mates, Dermot Clancy and his brother Kevin, who are big builders in London. Terry Wogan was at our table, and it was the first time I met him. We had a good chat and we promised each other a game of golf sometime. Who knows? I enjoyed myself to be honest. Had a few glasses of red wine, and a few glasses of Uncle Arthur. Ian Robertson was the main speaker and he was as witty as ever.

But then we had a big rush to get to Heathrow, and we bumped into the English boys who were on the same flight as us to Johannesburg. Rob Andrew and myself had to hang around the door of the 'plane for 10 or 15 minutes and shake hands a dozen times, the usual stuff two players end up doing when television crews have nothing better to do with themselves. Did the English boys not look pretty in their pink shirts!

Anyhow, despite the delay, I managed to park myself in first class. About 14 players in all made it to the top of the 'plane. I had to be there. I told Noisy that my ankle was swollen and I was going to need a lot of room!

In first class I have all the room I desire. What style! Jason Leonard and Dean Richards are beside us. We're chatting and having a bit of fun. I'm not going to drink anything. Just a glass of wine to help me nod off for a couple of hours.

Brian Moore waltzed up the aisle and did not seem too amused at seeing us all, in all our comfort. He's down at the back of the 'plane. Poor Brian. He gives us all a hard time before turning on his heels, and pretending he is mad. By the end of this flight, Brian is going to have a very sore rear end having been squeezed into that little seat of his for what will seem like a week and a half.

I suppose people looking at the Irish team from a distance have enough reason to imagine we are heading straight for a large disaster. We did not set the championship alight this season. Then we went out to northern Italy, about a week ago, for a World Cup warm-up and after the game the only part of our bodies which looked warm were our faces. Italy beat us. The first time they beat one of the International board teams. Beat us 22-12. Apparently they did a lap of honour at the end of the game.

We had an understrength team out and we had only flown out for the game the previous day, but I am not making excuses. Italy are a damn good team. We took them lightly, and if we had known that they had done something like 21 days in training camp in the run-up to the game then we might have had a different attitude. I can tell you that we have a different attitude about the Italians now. Watch them! They're a smart team.

They got the only try of the game early in the second-half and we were out on our feet by then. After the match, we had a full week of training set up in Kilkenny, but we could have done with a week before the game in Trevisio as well.

That game is out of our system now. It took a couple of days in Kilkenny to get over it. That's also a couple of days virtually wasted! That is the cost of losing to Italy. A ridiculous price to have to pay, though the remainder of the week in Kilkenny went very well. There was a lot of good work done. Good, fast work, in the bloody rain. We thought we might need the Ark to get out of the place.

As you know, we lost to England, Scotland and France in the championship. England was just a bad performance from us, and a tight, solid effort from them. Their pack won the day and made up for the sickeners of the two previous years. We were rotten bad in the second-half against Scotland at Murrayfield, and the French match was a non-event. It was all fairly depressing, to be honest, but it could have been worse. We could have been in the boots of the Welsh team at the finish of the championship.

At least, we beat them in Cardiff. Again at the Arms Park! And we play them again on June 4 in our final group game in the World Cup at Ellis Park in Johannesburg. Whether beating them in Cardiff was a good thing or a bad thing in the long run remains to be seen. It's going to make the Welsh mad as hell to beat us, we know that. But what good would losing to them in Cardiff have done?

At least we felt an awful lot better after winning that game. We didn't feel the worst team in the world! The Welsh team management of Alan Davies and Bob Norster were out on their ears after the match. It was important for us not to be torn apart, and it was equally important to keep up our winning record against them in their back garden. We did not want to lose that, in addition to getting the wooden spoon. There were lots of positive aspects to the victory.

I had a good afternoon myself, and I took advantage of Spencer John from Llanelli who was making his debut. I also went a few rounds with Phil Davies at the side of play early in the game, and I think I took that decision as well. The whole pack was brave and we forced them to turnover a lot of ball, which we didn't get much credit for the following morning. Ah, well! Fulcher and Tweedy did well in the lineout. Eric had to go off injured in the first-half, but Burkey came in and kicked 11 points. Good for him. Brennie won his 50th cap and scored his 17th try for Ireland, which also was not bad. Individually, every Irishman got his season up and running in the final game of the championship, and better late than never, especially with the World Cup around the corner.

It is absolutely vital that we reach the quarter-finals of the tournament. We have to beat Wales again. Ireland got to the quarter-finals of the previous two tournaments. We do not want to lose that foothold. We can not allow ourselves to slip further back down the mountain. I hear that some commentators have suggested that it would be better if we did land on our arses in the next few weeks, but what good would that do?

We are not asleep. The Irish team is working hard at its game, and even though improvement and consistency have both been hard to come by, it is totally daft to imagine that losing more games can help us. I don't understand their logic. I do not train and play rugby six night each week in order to lose games.

If we get to the World Cup quarter-finals, then we will know for sure that we have a base at which to work from, and see to it that the second-half of the 90s brings greater pride and ambition back into the Irish game. That is the long term target. First we have to beat Wales in two weeks time. It is one of the most important matches in the history of Irish rugby in my opinion, whether we beat the All Blacks in our opening game or not!

If we beat the All Blacks and Japan, we will still need to beat Wales just to make it absolutely certain that we go through to the quarters. Sure we might be the first Irish team to ever beat the All Blacks. Never know.

Now, I'm going to try to sleep for a while. I do not think I will have any trouble in this bed in the Heavens. I think I'll dream of Brian Moore and all the Micks squirming around behind me in their seats like overgrown sardines.

THURSDAY, MAY 18:

Arrived in Johannesburg and said goodbye to England. They had to travel on by coach to Durban where they are based to begin with. We're staying put, right here, and before we knew it we arrived at the Sunnyside Park Hotel, in a suburb called Braamfontein. It's a nice hotel, though a little bit small and we definitely will not get lost in it.

Straight away, we had a training session, which was supposed to be short and light. Giles Warrington, the team's fitness adviser, had warned us that training at altitude has to be built up on a gradual basis. We're 7,000 feet above sea level here. Even I will get the ball into touch, deep in the opposition's 22, if I decide to kick it! We trained in the Rand Afrikaans University, which is a very good facility, but it's an hour's journey by coach from the hotel. We were supposed to train in a ground around the corner from the hotel, but it has not got the names of the tournament sponsors surrounding the field. Money talks in this tournament.

We trained for two hours, and we all got a little bit carried away. Got back to the hotel, where I'm sharing with Tweedy to begin with. We have got six minders with the team. Every country has that number, and we also have two mini-buses and two cars at our disposal, but anybody who thinks of getting in behind the wheel will be sent home. The minders have to be with us everywhere we go, but with Davy Tweed stuck to my side I felt safe enough as it was.

Tweedy has not got a firearm, however, and each of the minders have. Johannesburg is a dangerous place according to reports and the information which has been given to us.

We trained again in the afternoon back at the University grounds and, at this rate of going, we will be spending about three hours per day on a coach going back and forward from the hotel to the ground. Noisy says he will look into it for us. It's not that we will have all that much to do with our time here. Our days will be made up of training and team meetings, lying on the bed, watching television, eating and eating and eating. If you are not very careful you can find yourself eating too much on a tour like this. You have nothing else to do. You eat out of boredom. Next thing, you're a stone up. I'm not going to wander down that road. There will be no red meat for me on this trip, for starters. No alcohol (well not very much alcohol) either.

We have a lot of work to do on the training field in the 10 days or so before the All Blacks match. We have to sharpen up on a lot of things after Kilkenny, and get some patterns going. We need a buzz in training which we can transfer into our matches.

That's going to be the problem for the first couple of days. We want to get down to it, but Giles has warned us about the sickness which will come by over-exerting ourselves early on. Some of us know what he is talking about. Before the last World Cup, during Ireland's short tour of Namibia, we lashed into it on the training field and the whole lot of us were dying from altitude sickness. In Namibia we trained hard for three days solid, and that was the end of the tour!

I met John Robbie in the hotel when we got back, another former Greystones boy! We have places and people to talk about. I discovered there is a Guinness bar in the hotel as well, ho ho? I hope I get to visit it before the World Cup is over. Not now. Now I am going to fall into my bed.

FRIDAY, MAY 19:

Decided to do the manly thing this morning, and take a morning dip! But the water in the pool was bloody freezing. The manageress of the hotel is there to witness this great specimen of Irish manhood in the water. She dipped her foot in and said it was perfect. My little finger told me it was not perfect. Too embarrassed to retreat, I jump in and jump out again, and make a mad, wet dash for it through the hotel in my swimming togs. I will not be starting my day off like this for the remainder of the trip.

After training, we had a team meeting about things. Nobody has any big problems. Though we had a problem this morning. We had a flat tyre on the coach as we left the hotel for the morning training session. Good start to the World Cup. We are still holding back in training rather than charging through it. It is very hot, about 21 degrees I'm told, and gallons of water are necessary. Giles Warrington wants us to drink, drink, drink, and no better men.

Noel, in fairness to him, is on the ball with the coach journey to and from our hotel. Today we ate at the University and that shaved one and a half hours off our bus journey. Giles finds it hard today to get us off the field on time. Some of us ignore him, because we want to do that little something more, but Noisy ends up ordering us off. And he's the boss.

There is a story in a newspaper back home, we hear, that Gerry Murphy is out of the management picture. Could have fooled us. He was in front of me all day on the training field. Gerry is the boss on the field out here. Noel Murphy is the boss off the field. They have no problems in their roles.

Namibia is still haunting some of us, so we are being careful and Noel was being extra careful when he told us to 'Get off!'

We have two liason officers for the tournament. One white and one coloured. The white one is a bit of a dour old bastard. Anyone who can spot him twice in an hour gets a prize. We have christened him Charlie. He does not smile at that. The coloured officer is an alright sort. The organisers seem to be balancing numbers off the field now that Chester Williams has hobbled off the South African squad, and left the home country looking as white as it has looked for the last one thousand years. We have two bag men with us as well, one white and one coloured.

Tonight we had our last squad get together before the tournament ends for us hopefully in four weeks time, around the time of the final, back here in Johannesburg! You never know. We go to a place called the Waterfront. I have a few pints which go down well. There are a few absentees from the squad, and when we set up the players' court later on in the week (I'm going to be Judge Popplewell again) fines are going to have to be handed out. Franno, Geoghegan and Halpin (I can't believe Flounder was not there) will have to speak up for themselves. Not that it will help them!

I discover that the Irish journalists will have to mind themselves while they are in Johannesburg. They have been issued with security tips. Things like not to linger outside a hotel entrance, not to travel alone on public transport, and not to walk near any alleyways.

SATURDAY, MAY 20:

Wake up at 6.0 a.m. No swim, I'm nobody's fool. The

whole squad had to head to the airport for a flight to Cape Town this morning for the official World Cup launch. We all had to look our smartest, which is hard for Flounder and Tweedy but they try their best!

At the airport, there is a mess up on the ticket front. Sean Diffley, our media man, and Joe Doran, our physio, are told there is no room for them on the 'plane. The only two men who probably wanted to be at the launch! Giles is told to stay in the hotel as well. But when we get to the airport we find that there were seats for the three of them.

Diffo and Doran missed nothing, however. Believe me! At Johannesburg airport, we met up with the Scots, the Tongans, the French and the Ivory Coast.

The Ivory Coast have no official blazers, and Scott Hastings thinks they should become the Ivory Coats. Good one Scott, now take a little rest! We are all on the same 'plane. The French have shaved their heads for some reason. They must be very bored indeed! Noel Murphy overhears some of our boys weighing it up, to shave or not to shave? He settles the debate with a powerful 'No!' Noel can see them all getting sunburned and running around with red heads. As it is we have Gary Halpin, and Flounder's head is a match for six or seven bald Frenchmen anyday.

I see my old friend Armary, and we have a good chat. It's good to see him. During the day we also met a large selection of players from other countries, a few Aussies, a few All Blacks. Sean Fitzpatrick is in good spirits. All smiles. I wonder does he know something that we don't, though Sean Fitz is always easy to get on with.

We had arrived in Cape Town far too early and, in the pissing rain, we were taken on a depressing tour of the place. The shanty towns look worse than they do on the television pictures we get at home.

All day we didn't see very much else. We didn't even see Table Mountain, which is one of the world's great sights. We didn't see it in the air or on the ground. Some feat! Instead we saw this great, big tent in the middle of a vineyard called Groot Constantia or something like that. As we approached in our coach, we could see these four or five tents stuck together. Franno thought it was for the caterers. But, no, the 16 best rugby teams in the world and all the bigwigs in world rugby were all herded into this thing with the rain still bucketing down.

The roof of the tent was full of water, and every so often somebody got drowned. It was a bit of a lottery, and it was not wise to stand in the one spot for too long. A couple of the Aussies got drenched. But we all got pretty wet. The loos were in boxes 50 yards away from the tent and we had to race to them and try to get into them, and make it back to the tent which was ready to collapse. The ground underneath in the tent was very uneven. The food was poor. The speeches were too long. And to think that we have all been waiting, for months, to get to South Africa.

We all get our World Cup caps, but too late to keep our heads dry! Everybody was knackered on the one and a half hour flight back to Johannesburg. Then there was an hour's delay at the airport as our minders waited to get their guns back.

It was rumoured that we would train later in the day, but that thought went by the board thankfully. Some of the boys went out playing golf. Staples, Franno, Eric, Fulcher, Geoghegan and myself decided that the two pool tables in the hotel would mean less walking.

SUNDAY, MAY 21:

Up at 8.0 a.m. Go for a swim again. Freeze my arse off again! Half the squad went out golfing this morning. My half trained in a local gymnasium which, unbelievably, has 36,000 members. And not too many of them coloured! It costs something like 2,000 rand (about £400) for the year, but with the cost of living out here you are really talking about the equivalent of about £2,000.

Tweedy, Bell, Johns, McBride and myself head off to an adventure gold mine in the afternoon. I've decided that Davy Tweed should be known as Charlie for the rest of the trip. Remember Charlie, from 'Coronation Street', the trucker with the black cowboy hat whom Beth had a thing with? Spitting image of each other. Tweedy is not impressed. He works on trains at home. He also has this fascination with taking pictures of all things which do not move. He's just like Riggers (Brian Rigney) in the good old days. Another great man for taking pictures of absolutely nothing.

We go down into the mine and see how it works, and down there it's McBride's turn to get all excited. Denis is an engineer and he worked in a mine in Africa for 12 months. Didn't know that! I buy this big black cowboy hat for Tweedy. Now, if she is watching the World Cup, Beth will be able to see him.

The boys who went out playing golf have a story they are telling about this white golfer hitting a black caddie with his wayward drive. 'Good shot' somebody shouted. Unbelievable. I suppose it will take years for the old beliefs to get out of their system over here.

We had a team meeting at 6.0 p.m. And Charlie Tweed got his John Wayne hat! We trained at the university grounds around the corner afterwards, and we had a fantastic session. Everybody felt good and strong. The right tempo was there all the time in everything we did with the ball. It was just as well, because there were a good few television cameras watching, including one belonging to a New Zealand crew.

We are losing about half a stone in weight with each session, but it is easy to put it back on again. Giles is in control of things. No sweat, if you know what I mean?

MONDAY, MAY 22:

No swim this morning. I felt really sick, honest to God, and I had to go see the doc. We had another great session on the field, even though I got sick in the middle of it! In the afternoon, Gerry and Noisy had organised a scrummaging session against some local teams. I don't know how many teams. Every time I looked up, there appeared to be a different prop facing me. Still, we have only about three bad scrums out of about 30. Good stuff, even though I picked a bad day to get sick.

The more we see of Johannesburg the more we can guess what it's really like to live here in South Africa. In the plusher areas, there are swimming pools behind the gates, but the gates are nearly all locked tight. There are bars on the windows of the fanciest houses, and we are told there are all sorts of elaborate burglar alarms in operation.

A stone's throw in any direction there is serious poverty, and I don't mean the sort we see at home. Later on this week some of us are going to visit one of the townships, but we are told we will be in an armoured car. About seven million blacks still live in holes beside white cities. Cardboard houses, I am told, with no water, no electricity, nothing. It's all hard to believe at times. But then you just have to take a look at the six bruisers who are minding us while we're over here. They look ready for anything.

TUESDAY, MAY 23:

Attacked the water again this morning. I'm getting used to it now, even though it was the coldest day we've had yet. There was a lovely big fire on in the foyer of the hotel, that's how cold it was!

I have contacted a local agent to help organise a few functions for the team over the next week. The first will be on Thursday, the night after we play Japan in Bloemfontein. We're going to go to this pub cum nightclub for a couple of hours. 'Chariots of Fire', it's called, and it will be worth a few rand to the squad. Right now our World Cup kitty is at zero.

We had a late afternoon session, which went on all day. Far too long, and the good pace at the beginning of the session fizzled out. I also pulled my hamstring slightly, something I could have done without, and probably wouldn't have done if we had a shorter, sharper run out.

WEDNESDAY, MAY 24:

No swim. No training. I can not risk it with my hamstring still that bit tender. Next week is the big week with the All Blacks to start with and Wales at the end of it. I'm not expecting to play against Japan. Three games in eight days is one game too many.

Last year I was bothered by this hamstring injury all year long, and I have to give it every chance to go away this week. This morning the team selected for the All Blacks was announced. Franno and Staples are in for

Tweedy and O'Shea. Feel sorry for the lads, but it is going to be a long week and everybody is bound to get their opportunity to try and shine out here.

The boys do another one hour session which stretches into two hours. When Pa Whelan gets going, he finds it hard to stop. Geoghegan and myself spent the two hours in the stands, in the shade, with buckets of ice and we would both have preferred to be in the thick of the action. We have waited long enough for this World Cup, without also waiting around this week.

We played pool again for a couple of hours this evening. Absolutely nothing on on television. The worst television in the world, no shadow of a doubt. It was a cold night, and the hotel had a good fire going again. It was needed.

THURSDAY, MAY 25:

Too cold to swim this morning. We are getting our heart rate checked every morning by Giles, and mine is the highest! Whether that is good or very bad, I have absolutely no idea. We watched the All Blacks on video again, and each time we watch them they seem to be getting better.

Some of the boys went to Soweto in a police convoy. I didn't. I need to rest up this leg. They tell me it was interesting and depressing. The Irish fans are beginning to appear in the hotel in dribs and drabs, and Ivan Power has a group from Greystones due to arrive any day now. I'm looking forward to seeing them.

We had a team meeting at 6.0, and after it Franno and myself decided to get to hell out of the hotel for a change of scenery and food. Noel Murphy brought us to this fantastic fish restaurant. It's been a long time since I had lobster. It was beautiful, and so cheap. Fantastic.

But you can't help wondering about what the boys saw today on their excursion. It's over a year since Mandela came to power, and law and order everywhere seems to be under pressure. Mandela, they say, is just keeping everything together. Most of the bad stories and the political stuff is happening in Natal where Inkatha is holding out against the ANC.

You look around the place and you wonder why the World Cup is taking place here, but people here think the tournament can help the country. That would be a good thing. South Africa needs all the help it can get.

They are also looking for the Olympic Games in 2004. They have a long way to go before they are ready for that, but if this World Cup is a success, then who knows? Rugby was the white man's game here. Rugby and apartheid went together in the eyes of the blacks, and you can only wonder how they feel about the whole thing.

A lot of white people sleep with guns beside their beds, but we have been told that most of the murders and rapes are taking place in the townships where people are lucky to have a roof over their heads not to think about a high-tech alarm system.

The opening ceremony was held today, and the opening game between South Africa and Australia. Everybody seemed to enjoy themselves during the ceremony, Mandela most of all. He seemed to love it. The game was fantastic. The South Africans were so charged up and they deserved to win it. They had the wind in their sails.

The whites and blacks seemed to get on well together in the stadium, no problem. The newspapers have been telling us it would be like this. All week they have been talking about the 'Rainbow Nation', but when you take a look inside the newspapers, you just want to quickly shut them closed again. There are stories all over the place about murders, rapes and shootings. Last month there were over 200 people killed in Natal. There were over 200 policemen murdered in South Africa last year. It's all unbelievable when you look at South Africa and Australia in today's opening game of the World Cup. The stadium was a mass of fantastic colours. All the people were smiling at the cameras. It was a brilliant game. It was a great day for South Africa, I think, and hopefully they will have more good days like this on the way in the next few weeks.

The Afrikaners themselves are a bit hard to take however. I have to say that. As soon as they had beaten Australia, most of them in our hotel were behaving as though they had won the World Cup. They can be a big-headed lot. When you look at Louis Luyt, the president of South African rugby, and listen to some of the things he has said in the past, you would wonder what the white South African is really thinking?

The Springbok skipper, Francois Pienaar and Mandela are great mates on the face of it. It was good to see. The two African anthems before the game went on forever, but I suppose they had to keep everybody happy. The Black anthem, 'Nkosi Sikelel i Afrika', which I remember from a couple of old movies on apartheid, gets my vote. They can throw the other one, 'Die Stem', away whenever they feel it's safe to do so.

FRIDAY, MAY 26:

South Africa has a long way to go. You see photographs of the Springboks everywhere, on every wall, and every passing truck practically. But soccer is the game of the blacks. It just goes to show that the whites still have all the money to spend, I suppose.

No swim this morning. Halpin, Staples, Tweedy and myself went to a couple of schools to meet black kids and white kids, and sign a few footballs and help out with a bit of coaching. I, of course, have to put my big foot in it by rabbiting on at the poor school about the facilities in the rich school. It sounded awful. We went to Ellis Park to get a sniff of the place for tomorrow's game. The boys kicked a few balls and we did a few lineouts. The pitch was in brilliant shape, but it is always a bit eerie walking around the insides of an empty stadium.

This evening the team had a quick bite to eat and we went out to the cinema. We went to see 'The Shawshank Redemption', a bloody excellent movie. Good story about life prisoners, which was a good choice by Franno for a change.

Tomorrow is the day. Ireland and the All Blacks! We have looked at them on video for so long and talked about them for so long, that it will be good to actually get onto the same field as them. Tomorrow will be a relief in a way. We're ready for them. I think we can surprise them. The day will surely come when Ireland will beat New Zealand.

SATURDAY, MAY 27:

It did not happen. It could have happened, but it didn't. We gave away two stupid tries in the first-half and you can not do that against a team which makes virtually no mistakes. The brilliance of the All Blacks as a team is that they do not make a present of the ball or hand out any free gifts. We gave them two tries! To beat them we would have had to be flawless in our performance, from start to finish, no mistakes.

It was a long, long day, and with the game not starting until 8.0 p.m. it was a bit of a roller coaster ride from breakfast right up to kick-off. You get all charged up, and you try to calm yourself down, and then you start getting all charged up again.

We spent most of the morning playing pool, Staples, Halpin, Geoghegan, Franno, the same group. There's no real reason why we end up together, it's just the way it happens. The other highlight of the morning was Halpin's pipe theft. The one Irish journalist who really likes his pipe had it swiped, but we gave it back to him when he looked to be in a bad way after three or four hours.

We had lunch at 2.0 p.m., and we were still no nearer to heading to Ellis Park at the end of it. We were due to be leaving for Bloemfontein at 7.0 a.m. tomorrow but Noisy has told us he has booked a flight four hours later instead. At the time we were hoping for a bit of a late night and a lie-in sounded like a good idea.

We watched England against Argentina. They had a hard time of it, and they really needed Rob Andrew doing his stuff with the penalties, but it was hard for us watching the game. It was hard to have any interest in it. We were watching England against Argentina, but Ireland and the All Blacks were already playing in our heads. We met up again at 6.0 p.m. and left the hotel 20 minutes later.

There was a police escort, but it was decided against using the flashing lights on the way to the stadium. That is usually counter-productive. It can leave everybody pumped up and in a bit of a sweat, and most of the boys, me especially, like to prepare ourselves for the game in a calm and collected fashion in the last couple of hours.

We were at the ground far too early, and we spent a long time on the field. The support, however, even one hour before the match, was incredible. There was so much green all over the place. Before we knew it we were listening to the new Irish pre-game anthem and we were looking at them doing the Haka.

It is hard to believe now that we lost the game by 24 points. It was a wrong score, 43-19, but nobody is going to write 'wrong score' down in the record books when the game is put away. In years to come it will probably appear to be another Irish stuffing. It wasn't like that. We played for the full 80 minutes. We stayed with them the whole way, and tonight they will know the victory was not as easy as it already looks. They know that. We know it. It's a pity.

But we made three or four big mistakes, and you can't do that against them. Halpin also made the mistake, after scoring our first try and putting us into the lead after a few minutes, of giving them the fingers. You don't do that anywhere and you certainly do not do it in the face of the All Blacks, but I know it was a spur of the moment thing from Gary. He was so charged up. He had just scored and Sean Fitz said something naughty to him. Next thing he's got the fingers up, and we're trying to pull him back.

It was still a great start. The rest of the game was tough, and the Aussie referee made it tougher for us the longer the game went on. I hate giving out about refs, and I really hate giving out about Australian refs because they are usually hopeless. The first test between the Lions and the All Blacks two years ago, we had one of these Aussie refs! Tonight we had another one. This guy had one set of rules for them and one set of rules for us. It would not have been too bad if we could have swapped the different sets at half-time or something like that. It's not funny. He was tearing our hearts out with his decisions.

Making excuses, after playing against Jonah Lomu, is probably not very clever. What can I say about the new boy in the All Blacks team? There had been so much talk about him for the last week, being ten feet tall and 20 stones or something! But you don't listen to it. We didn't talk about Lomu much either.

We thought he was just another All Black, but he is most definitely very special. We gave him the first try when Mick Bradley hacked the ball straight into his hands after a ruck about 20 yards from our line. That was just bad luck.

Staples is out of the tournament after breaking his finger. That is so unfortunate for him. It was the same story for him in the last World Cup. He is so unlucky. Philip Danaher is being flown in as his replacement.

We were in front of them almost up to half-time, and we probably needed to reach half-time in that position if we were to really set ourselves up for a big second-half. The second-half was good, but we were chasing them after Lomu's try. Brennie had his kick blocked down by Bunce after that and, out of nothing, they led by 13 points. It looked all wrong on the scoreboard, and it definitely did not reflect what had happened on the field.

We could have thrown in the towel. We did not, thankfully! Geoghegan made a run down the left wing, and Bell and Bradley were in support, and McBride got in for a try after the ball went loose on their line. Eight points down at half-time. We should have been eight in front, because Eric had missed with a couple of kicks, as well as us handing them the two tries. I had to have a piss at half-time in the middle of the field, which was a bad idea because coming off the field after the game, I was pulled in to do a drugs test.

All their new boys did well. The out-half, Mehrtens, is a cool customer. He has good pace and he kicked the ball well all night. Kronfeld, their new wing forward, is useful. And the rest of the team was the same as usual. Jones was good in the lineout, and Sean Fitz had them going well in the loose play.

They were the better team in the second-half, the same as we had been the better team in the first-half. Lomu destroyed us with one run. The boys just bumped off him. At least Corkery's try raised our spirits at the end. That would have been the right way to end the match. It would have been only fair, but their full-back, Osborne, ended up getting the final try of the game.

We should not have let him in for that try. We needed to finish the game on the highest note possible and it would have also been nice not to lose by over 20 points. Still, everybody seemed happy enough after the game.

Apart from me. I had to wait an hour and a half to get a precious 100 millilitres out of my system, and at that he let me away with giving a little under the minimum requirement. I had to give Olo Brown, their tight head, a Baa-baas jersey I'd promised him two years ago, so I was a busy boy after the match running in and out of different rooms.

Our pack did well, I thought, for the whole game. We kept it together and never panicked for about 95% of the match. Brown and myself had our usual tussle. He's a good player and a good bloke, but I think we'll be glad not to bang into one another for another couple of years. It was a hard bloody game. When we got back to the hotel, I was not able to eat that much. I was told I am playing against Japan on Wednesday, so that meant I wasn't drinking either. I struggled through four or five cans of Coke and went to bed early. I was due to meet some of the Greystones boys, but they were late, and I was too tired to hang around.

We are all happy enough with today. The press seemed happy too. It's just the 20 points which is pissing me off. It was not a true scoreline. I still have to pack bags for tomorrow. Oh, Lord.

SUNDAY, MAY 28:

Stiff and sore, and beginning to feel the effects of last night's game, I still had to tidy up the room to a reasonable degree first thing this morning. We don't want anybody to think there was a litttle piggy in the house, do we?

We had the entire 'plane to ourselves on the flight down to Bloomers. Bloemfontein! It was a short journey, about an hour, which was just as well because every man who played last night is suffering in some way. At the airport, we were met by a school band. And Tweedy grabs this great big drum (he was in some band in Belfast as a boy) and he gives a little performance. None of us bother thanking him or throwing him a few coppers.

We are staying in a Holiday Inn this time. I'm rooming with Wally (Paul Wallace) and it looks like he will be winning his first cap against the Japs. After half an hour's kip, which was needed, we had lunch in the Hard Rock Cafe in the hotel. The food was terrible and very hard to eat.

The afternoon session was long enough. Too long, to be honest! If I was having my way out here I would be doing everything in shorter sessions and looking to get things sharp. Get things right, and then leave it. They are my thoughts, but then I am the loose head prop and who is going to listen to little old me?

We watched last night's match after the session, and it's hard to say how the boys felt about it. It was definitely a lost opportunity in many respects, though it was a good performance. The sort of performance we were aiming for really. If we had just cut out those three or four mistakes, you never know? We might have been there at the finish.

Gareth Edwards is staying in our hotel, and I had a good chat with him. He thinks we did an awful lot right against the All Blacks, but he fancies Wales to come out of the group. He honestly does. It has been hard for us to seriously think about the Welsh while the All Blacks were in our path. Now they are out of our way, and here we are down here getting ready for Japan.

Three games in eight days is hard going on the mind and body, switching on and switching off different teams. We have given the least amount of thought to Japan and, hopefully, we will be able to take them in our stride between the two weekend matches.

MONDAY, MAY 29:

First thing this morning I was called in by Noisy into the team meeting room. Pa was already there. I was trying to quickly think of what I had done wrong, had I paid my room bill at the last hotel? What had I broken? Did I open my mouth too wide to the press?

I was asked would I like to captain Ireland against Japan on Wednesday? I took about half a second to tell them that that would be alright.

It's fantastic news for me. I had been asked last year

about the captaincy, but I was after coming back from knee surgery and I felt it would not be on. It was bad timing, and I've wondered several times since if I would ever regret putting a wet blanket over the idea?

The team was later announced, and Wally is in! Unfortunately, other players like Henry Hurley and Anthony Foley are not going to get matches during this tournament it would appear. Henry is very disappointed. He can not hide it, and why should he? Unless I get injured, God forbid, I am also going to be playing against Wales and hopefully whatever match follows in the quarter-final.

I had a good chat with Terry. He is very supportive, as I knew he would be. I told him I am only keeping the seat warm for him. If Woody has a stormer against Japan, which is something he is capable of doing (he could just go mad and run in tries all over the shop), then Terry might be in an uncomfortable position. Knowing Terry, he will wish us both the very best, come what may!

Halpin tells me my picture will now be up on the wall in Lansdowne Road, and he slags me off about how I'll look like an old fart. I don't mind how I look, as long as he is forced to genuflect in front of me every time he plays a match in the ground.

A lot of fines and interesting forms of punishment were handed out in court last night. Most are unmentionable, however. I'm sorry. Wally had to sing a song because he is winning his first cap, which is normal enough, but once he began we realised that it was not a smart idea. Normally a new captain has also to get up onto his feet and give a burst of some tune. I was not asked. A few of the boys must have heard me spontaneously breaking out one night. Danaher has arrived on the tour, replacing

Staples, and he instantly received a whole hatful of fines for missing the first 11 days out here. Serves him right.

There is a good spirit in the squad now, though I have found that there is a bit of a strain between myself and Henry. I know he is disappointed about not playing on Wednesday, but it is quite obvious that the two of us have had nothing to say to one another. I am going to have to do something about that at the first opportunity.

TUESDAY, MAY 30:

Bits and pieces took up the morning, like an interview with John Robbie on the radio, and the official tour photograph was also taken. Robbie has done well for himself since coming out here in 1981. He is well thought of as a broadcaster, and as a player he actually made it to the Springboks replacement bench which was quite an achievement.

Paul Burke and Niall Hogan went through all the patterns they want to do tomorrow against Japan. The pair of them will be running the game, not me! They will have to make most of the decisions on the field when I, hopefully, will have myself buried in rucks and mauls. After that we visited the ground, the Free State Stadium, which was built only seven months ago we are told in time for the World Cup. It's a super ground, though just walking around it we were suffering a little from the heat. It is fierce hot down here.

The Holiday Inn is no holiday (they never are!), and Halpin, Franno, Mullin and myself go out for some ribs. We should not have bothered. Awful things! At least it got us out of the hotel for a couple of hours, even if we did return a hungry bunch. We had done our lineout practice at the ground while we were there, so we had the entire afternoon to ourselves. Most of us rest up. It's important on a tour like this not to be running around the place. Sitting around gets boring, but sometimes it has to be done.

We all went to an Italian restaurant for dinner, and it was only superb. The place was candle-lit and very dark, and I thought it was a good idea to pour some wax into one or two desserts. Nobody came to any harm. We don't want anybody getting sick the night before the game, do we?

An early night. I'll be in the bed by 10 o'clock.

WEDNESDAY, MAY 31:

Now all we have to think about is Wales. In our hearts, we always knew it would come down to this, Ireland or Wales for the second placed spot in the group? It is a big relief to have Japan behind us. It was always going to be a game we needed to win and get out of the way. No disrespect to the Japanese, but we were always going to have some difficulty knuckling down for this game. Ireland are not brilliant when we are in the odds-on favourites role. We are usually much better when we have our backs to the wall. It suits our nature more, I think, to be fighting an uphill battle.

Today's game was uphill and downhill, as it turned out. We came close enough to making a mess of it. We won 50-28 in the end, and the Japanese probably feel the same way right now as we felt last Saturday after going down by the same sort of margin to the All Blacks.

The day got off to a surprising start. Something I did not need as I was trying to concentrate fully on the game and on my own role as captain. Noisy called me into one of the rooms in the hotel this morning and told me that

the do I have organised for tomorrow night in Johannesburg is taking place in a strip joint.

It was a total surprise to me. I didn't know anything
about any strippers. The agent I had contacted out here
had set the whole thing up. The place is called 'Chariots
of Fire', and the Irish team was due to call into the place
for a couple of hours, have a few beers and leave. It was
going to be a big do. They were expecting about 3,000
people to show up. But I was not expecting strippers.

Noisy told me there was an advertisement in the newspapers which had the strippers and the Irish team in the
same place. I told him that I would see to the matter. I
had to make a few telephone calls and try to cancel the
thing. I told the agent we could not be associated with the
whole thing. I don't know if they understand or not. It's
a pity the thing has to be cancelled. A lot of organisation
went into it and we would have made a good few bob for
our kitty.

I had been told the place was one of the biggest bars in
the world, and not a strip joint. We probably would not
have even seen one stripper if we went. But, maybe not.
The way our luck goes with these sort of things a stripper
would have landed on the lap of an Irish player with a
beer in his hand, and there would probably be a photog-
rapher just in the right place to capture the smiling couple! We would have looked right eejits.

Strippers or no strippers, once the advertisement has
appeared we now have to walk away from it. People
would try to put things together, and next thing there
would be rumours that the Irish boys have been out on
the piss all week long.

We had a meeting at 1.10 p.m.. I know that, because
captains have to know these things! Seriously, I had spent
half an hour preparing myself for the captain bit. It is not

something that I have had that much experience with. I captained Leinster a few times, but not that often. The talk went well. I felt comfortable in the role. We arrived at the ground too early and we had a lot of time standing around doing nothing. That was the only problem.

Everybody seemed switched on, and ready for the game. I won the toss. Good start! I let them play with the sun into their eyes for the first-half, and we had everything going our way for the opening quarter or so. We had 19 points on the board before we knew it. It was a dream start. Apart from the fact that Woody did his shoulder in and had to leave the field. It looks very bad for him. He looks out of the tour, and he might be a long time out of the game trying to get himself right. We all feel very sorry for him. He is such a strong and brave player, but he will still have a long career with Ireland I hope.

Terry replaced Woody, and he also took over the captaincy role which is normal procedure. I led Ireland for less than 20 minutes! It's a bit like the day I won my first cap for Ireland against the All Blacks, when I had to leave the field after eighteen and a half minutes. Same story almost, except luckily enough it was not me leaving the field this time.

Corkery, Franno and Geoghegan scored our tries early on, and it felt that little bit too easy. I think we relaxed slightly. Maybe our concentration dropped or something, but at the same time they came storming back at us and there was only five points in it at half-time.

In the second-half we had a right battle on our hands most of the time. We had trouble getting possession. Our lineout ball dried up. We were in some difficulties. It was not that we did not know what to expect from them. We played Japan in the World Cup four years ago and we

Davy Tweed (left) and David Corkery in full battlecry before we played Japan in South Africa. Or are they rehearsing for the pub later on?

Gary Halpin, Terry Kingston and myself, with the World Cup in front of us (above) and Halpin letting the All Blacks know what he thinks of them (bottom) after scoring our opening try of the tournament.

I do my Jonah Lomu impression (above) against the All Blacks, and the real thing (below) gets the full attention of Corkery, Denis McBride, Maurice Field and Paddy Johns.

Playing the captain's part, before meeting Japan in Bloemfontein, with Eddie Halvey (left) and Paul Wallace

Myself and Geoghegan are not amused at sitting in the shade, nursing ourselves, as the boys sweat it out on the field below us.

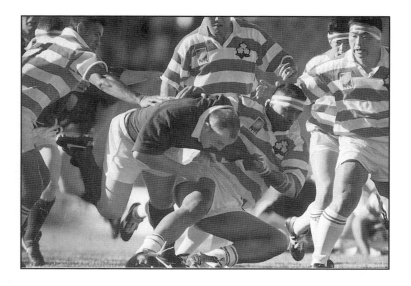

Keith Wood bites the dust with the encouragement of half the
Japanese pack (above) and Denis McBride eludes the entire Welsh
pack to score our second try in the deciding group game in the
tournament.

Eric Elwood lends a hand at a training camp in one of the South African townships.

Wally, Woody and Poppy! Hard at work on the training field in South Africa.

Halpin a.k.a. Flounder the fish, in his natural habitat (above) and yours truly (below) saying hello to the Indian Ocean in Durban.

Praise the Irish fans! We do our lap of honour after beating Wales in Ellis Park. Mission accomplished!

knew the kind of game they have been playing since then. We did not expect it to be easy. Against the Welsh they had been unfortunate with the bounce of the ball on more than one occasion, and I think they saw this afternoon's game as their only possible salvation in the World Cup.

They gave it everything. They had real pace all over the field, and even though they lacked the power to back it up they had sufficient homework done to trouble us in the set pieces. In the lineout they had lots of clever variations. For 20 minutes we seemed to be doing nothing but chasing shadows. But we stuck at it. We dominated the game when it mattered.

Any time things got too close for comfort we were able to pull away from them. We also scored seven tries, which is not to be scoffed at. Two of them were penalty tries. We really had their scrum in trouble on their own line and they were forced to collapse several times. There is no point ignoring the fact, however, that we spilled far too much good ball and we did not put in tackles at times when they simply had to be made. We have a lot of work ahead of us in the next four days before we play Wales on Sunday.

It was not a good game. We did not have a good night either. We were brought to the Irish Ambassador's place for what turned out to be a long, long, long night! The poor Japanese were there, and with little English between them, at least they were in a better position than the Irish team who had to listen to an awful lot of stuff we had absolutely no interest in.

We watched Wales playing New Zealand in our hotel before leaving for the ambassador's do, and they did pretty well for a while. It's down to the two of us now! I have to admit we have had Wales at the back of our

minds ever since we beat them in Cardiff in the final
game in the championship.

THURSDAY, JUNE 1:

I wonder what the girls are doing with themselves
tonight, now that they don't have to take their clothes off!
I really could have done without this stripper business. It
puts me under pressure in the middle of a week when I
do not need anything extra on my mind. I have been told
that the I.R.F.U. are supportive, but I am still worried
about the whole thing. The failure of the Irish team to
turn up, after we had been booked into the place, could
lead to some trouble. I hope not. I would just like to forget all about the entire business.

As for organising something else for our World Cup
kitty, forget about it! I've had enough. I had a drink with
Doran and Diffo (physio Joe Doran, and press officer
Sean Diffley) this evening. The two wise men of the Irish
group! We had a laugh about the whole thing, and it was
good to get their thoughts on the whole affair. Diffo is
merciless when it comes to having a laugh at someone's
expense, like me for instance!

We had a quick team meeting about R.T.E. today. We
have been reliably informed that their rugby panel has
been slagging us off once again. We have learned to live
with their criticism over the years, but there are occasions
when they can be extremely negative and hurtful. And it
can be hard to take! We have decided to let them say
what they want to say in Dublin. We are going to do what
we have to do out here. We don't want to think about
R.T.E. So we have also decided not to talk to them either.

They always want total access to the Irish team and
usually we oblige them. But we have now decided that if

they want to interview players they can talk to the Japanese and the Welsh, and the All Blacks if they can catch up with them. It is hard on the R.T.E. boys on the ground out here, because they are supportive and decent towards us, but that is the decision which has been taken.

No interviews! It is not something which we wish to build into a major issue, because we stopped losing sleep over R.T.E.'s criticism a long time ago.

Travelling from Bloemfontein back to Johannesburg, or travelling anywhere around this country, it makes you think about the whole South African situation. And forget about rugby for a few hours. God love the blacks here! They must have come through hell in this country, and even still at least 10 inequalities hit you in the face every single day.

It's bad enough for the people to be getting a rough time from the whites over the years. But, in the last 10 years alone, over 20,000 people have been killed in the political fighting between supporters of the African National Congress (Mandela's party) and Chief Buthelezi's Inkatha Freedom Party. We have had the Northern Ireland situation at home, but this seems a huge tragedy out here. It all looks very sad.

The blacks in Bloemfontein appeared to exist on a different planet to the whites and us tourists. All over this country almost 10 million children live in poverty. It is hard to fully comprehend those sort of figures. Really believe them. We see the fantastic game parks and the beautiful scenery, and we hear about the beaches, and you wonder how these two vastly different situations can exist side by side. I read one article in a newspaper which said 12 million people are without clean water, and 21 million people don't have proper sanitation. Nine million people are in squatter camps.

Nelson Mandela has only had one year in power, but with all the problems out here, where does he start? In Johannesburg, we checked into another Holiday Inn. How can we complain? We have food, a roof over our heads, windows and curtains, carpets! The one thing about Holiday Inns is that they are all the same. Once you walk through the front door of the hotel you have no idea where you are anymore, what city or what country? But we are not moaning.

There was another crowd of singers outside the hotel ready to entertain us as soon as we got down off the coach. We were waiting around listening to them, when I noticed a gardener watering some plants with a hose. I asked him for it and I turned it on some of our boys, but I think I half-drowned Henry Hurley. He did not look amused.

Shane Byrne from Blackrock has arrived out as cover for Woody. Byrne is a good, strong player and he has a great attitude to the game. If only he'd get himself a haircut! It is two minutes from the hotel to the training ground, which is perfect. Myself, Franno and Gary were at the back of the bunch on the field, and Noisy made it his business to tell us to get our act together. I try. My legs are shagged.

A quick swim and a sauna was needed at the end of the day. I did a couple of interviews with some Welsh reporters. We received our daily allowance from Noisy and hit the sack.

FRIDAY, JUNE 2:

We trained at a local school, and we put a decent session under our belts. Later Halpin, McBride, Terry, Eric and myself went to a flea market where I met a lot of

Wexford boys from back home. We haggled our heads off all day in the market and bought rakes of stuff. God only knows how we are going to get it all home with us. All the stuff was so cheap.

Two days to go to Wales. It would be dreadful to have to go home on Monday. It would be a disaster. The difference between finishing in the top eight in the world and finishing just outside the top eight is huge. This next game will have a big bearing on all of our careers, and it is not being over-dramatic to imagine it as the most important game we might ever play.

The tension is already building up within the squad.

SATURDAY, JUNE 3:

The boys who were expecting us at their pub last Saturday night have been good about the whole mix-up. There is going to be no hassle at all. Went shopping with Halpin this morning, in another effort to escape our hotel basically, and I met up with Jim Casey and Frank Deering and some of the boys from Gorey. A nice surprise. Small world. We also spotted the Aussie ref who was not very kind to us in the game against the All Blacks last Saturday night.

We thought up all sorts of things we could do to him, from kidnapping him right down to some amusing little prank, but in the end we decided that we might see him again in an official capacity before this tournament ends. We behave like gentlemen towards him. In other words, we totally ignore him.

Halpin gets me to buy a pair of Roman Docs which I will never, ever wear, but he makes me put them on there and then, and we look like Mutt and Jeff walking around the place.

Niall Hogan had his graduation ceremony in the hotel, from the Royal College of Surgeons in Dublin! His parents and his family were out here for it and they had a very proud day. Now we have got Hogan to cut us up. We have Paddy Johns to look after our teeth (he's a dentist), and the next thing we need is a physio. If the I.R.F.U. keep this squad together they will make huge savings on future tours. I'm kidding! Ken Reid spoke at the ceremony for Niall, and I like Ken! We've had good times together, but he was speaking as president of the I.R.F.U. and, in my book, he picked the wrong time and the wrong place to give a big speech on the value and importance of amateurism.

It was Niall's big day, and he and the rest of us have to play Wales tomorrow in one of the biggest matches of our careers. Most of the boys were very disappointed to hear Ken go on and on.

I had a good chat with Staples, who is very disappointed at having to leave the tournament halfway through it. He will hang around until tomorrow and then head back to England on Monday. It must be heart-breaking to have to leave the team behind like this.

We had a team meeting at 2.30 p.m. and we went through every aspect of the game for tomorrow afternoon. We watched the Welsh match against the All Blacks again, and picked up a few more things. Then we watched the Scots being beaten by France in their final group game. Really Scotland gave the French the match, and for their sins they will now be playing the All Blacks in the quarter-finals.

The French will face the winners of Ireland and Wales. Nobody in our party wants to think about that this evening. Tonight's movie was 'Bad Boys', and it was not bad, not good. Okay just. We were back in the hotel at

10.30. And it was straight to bed, though we chatted and sat and talked on the way. Everybody is so nervous and uptight about the match. Sleep might not come that easily to most of us tonight.

SUNDAY, JUNE 4:

Next Saturday afternoon Ireland will play France in Durban. We are into the quarter-finals of the World Cup! It is hard for me to fully explain how I feel and how all the boys feel. This has been a long, emotional, draining day. We beat Wales by one point, 24-23, I believe. It sounds good to me. Most of all, I think, there is a massive relief in our hotel tonight.

An awful lot of people told us we would not have a ghost of a chance in this World Cup. They were not saying this to us directly, but all around us that is what was being said. Not that all that talk matters a damn now. The people who matter tonight are the members of the Irish team and our management, and the thousands and thousands of supporters who made Ellis Park Ireland's property this evening. They came from all over Ireland and they came from all over Africa as well, and fair dues to them. We have those people to thank very especially for this victory.

We did that after the game. Halpin and myself thought it would be a good idea to go on a lap of honour. We danced our way around the field. The crowd lapped it up, and we lapped it back! It was fantastic. Our dream has been realised and we deserved to celebrate in style. On the way around, I saw John Rochford, Pat Garvey, Luke McKeever and Brendan Donnelly and, incredibly, I was able to make arrangements to meet up with them afterwards. We met up in O'Hagan's, a nice pub half a mile down the road from our hotel.

All morning there had been supporters milling in and out of the hotel, and it felt just like Dublin on a Saturday morning. Except the tension was double that of anything I have experienced with Ireland before.

Everybody must have been feeling the pressure in our hotel, including the boys in the kitchen, because for breakfast they served us bowls of spaghetti bolognese. As if we wanted to be reminded of our Italian experience before the start of this World Cup! We all shifted ourselves to the main dining room, where we had pancakes.

More confusion raised its head on the ticket front. I hate having to think about tickets on the morning of a match, but I had left tickets for some boys from Greystones in our hotel and they were missing this morning. It took an hour or so before they were located.

I went into a sports shop nearby and bought some gear for David, my kid brother at home. You never know, just in case I ended up going home tomorrow! We did some lineout practice at 1.0 o'clock. It was very hot. Back in the hotel we had our team meeting. As usual, we got to the ground far too early. I did my customary two laps. I saw Frank Deering and Pascal Whitmore in one corner of the stadium and they had a Gorey flag with them. They shouted at me to score a try in their corner so all the folks in Ireland would see them. I said 'Sure I will!'

What happened in the first few minutes of the game? Yours truly scores the opening try of the match! But I go over in the wrong corner, and I will have to apologise to the boys the next time I see them!

It was a good try. I got the ball about 40 yards out in the middle of the pitch and I sidestepped two or three Welsh players before sprinting over in the right corner. Naw! It wasn't exactly like that. There was this lineout three yards from their line. I took the ball off Paddy Johns and put the head down! We were 14-0 up before we knew it. Denis McBride scored the try I wanted to score. He drove forward from a maul about 40 yards out and he went through the entire Welsh pack. They appeared to stop him, but he wriggled free and made it under the Welsh posts all on his own. We were thinking to ourselves 'What's going on here?' I don't know what the Welsh boys must have been thinking.

I can recall only one bad scrum from us during the entire match, and that was when I tried to take John Davies on, on the outside. I ended up slipping out of the scrum and they drove us back about 30 yards. We won the game by a lot more than one point in reality. Hemi Taylor scored a try for them about half an hour into injury time. My legs were gone by then. We were all at a virtual standstill.

Geoghegan and Jonny Bell brought off two great tackles in the first-half which really stopped the Welsh in their tracks the only time they looked like taking us on. In the first-half they also scored with a dropped goal which was illegal. The ball went to their outhalf Adrian Davies straight from a free-kick, and even loose head props know you can not do that!

That score upset us a bit. It knocked our concentration, but not for too long. At half-time we were eight points up on them. Corkery was playing brilliantly, yet again (what a tournament he is having) and Paddy Johns and McBride were everywhere. Franno and Fulcher won good lineout ball. Halpin, Terry and myself, well, what can I say? We did pretty well.

Halvey came in for McBride in the second-half and scored almost immediately, and with 10 minutes to go there was 12 points in it. Their hooker, Jonathan Humphreys, took advantage of our tired legs to go in for a try, but Eric kicked a penalty to leave us clear again. It was a long wait for the final whistle however. Too bloody long.

The Welsh tactics were not the smartest I have ever witnessed and they never looked like troubling us, but to think that if we didn't get that late penalty and if Taylor had still scored his late try, we might have been knocked out of the tournament. Ifs do not matter now. It would have been a travesty if we had lost. We were in control of the game from beginning to end, and they spent most of the game taking long drop-outs which we belted back at them with interest.

We came out here to qualify. Now we have done that. The big effort has been worthwhile. We feel on top of the world, even though there are seven other teams still in the tournament keeping us company. R.T.E. were screaming for interviews after the game. We said 'No thank you'. It would have been easy to say 'Yes. Sure thing.' A decision is a decision, and we all had to stand by it.

Mentally, as much as physically, this match was a cup final situation for us, and that is why we did the lap of honour even though we had no trophy to bring around with us. The Welsh are going home. We are staying here. Better still, we are going to Sun City tomorrow for a couple of days R and R. It was a quick decision on the part of Noel Murphy, courtesy of the I.R.F.U.

Fair dues to the union. Two days with the feet up is what we all need. Tonight in the hotel we had a brief meeting. There was not that much to say, however, because nobody is capable of thinking about the French tonight. In O'Hagan's pub, I met up with Rochford and Co., the Gorey boys, and a lot of people who always believed in us and always thought it worthwhile following us to Africa.

By the time I was heading to my bed, there were Welsh supporters pouring into our hotel. Rather than go home, they have decided to switch allegiance to us. That's what they were saying. I hope they do stick around, because we might need all the help we can get from here on in.

MONDAY, JUNE 5:

There was a team meeting at 9.30 this morning to say good-bye to Woody and Staples. I feel sorry for the two boys. What a time to be going home? Leaving us behind in the quarter-finals of the World Cup, with the hard work over and the interesting stuff just beginning. Not that the French on Saturday will not be hard! They will be themselves. But I think they are the team we would have chosen to meet next if it had been left up to us. On the evidence of the tournament to date, the Scots would have appeared a more difficult assignment. The French are getting things right and wrong, and they have a big problem with their half-back pairing.

We left the two boys in our hotel, and headed off on a two hours journey by coach to the holiday resort of Sun City. Things could always be worse for Woody and Staples. They could be going home in a bad way, like Max Brito of the Ivory Coast. I cannot remember what Brito looked like, but we had met up with them on the day we went down to Cape Town for the launch of the tournament. Brito has been left a quadriplegic after injuring himself in a ruck or maul against Tonga last Saturday.

Brito lives in the south of France. He's an electrician, and he has a wife and two children. It is a real tragedy for them. But it is one which affects us all. Everybody is talking about him and thinking about him. An injury like that is everyone's worst fear. We can only wish him the best, and hope and pray for some sort of recovery, even though it is unlikely. I didn't see the incident, but seemingly it was a freakish thing.

It is something, to be honest, which you try not to think about for too long. What good can that do? The people out here are going to open some kind of trust in his name. That is the best thing to do right now.

Trying to forget about Max Brito and arriving in Sun City, we were stunned by what we found. This place is the mecca of gambling down here. It is so wealthy looking. The hotel we are staying in is the most palatial place I have been in. I have travelled the world with a rugby ball and this place is unbelievable. Outrageous really! Minding our Ps and Qs will be of the utmost importance for the couple of days we are here. The hotel itself is not that expensive. About £120 for a room for two people for one night, but that is because of the cost of living out here. There is a man-made beach here. Man-made waves, and loads of slides and stuff. Brad and the boys head for the golf course straight away. I collapse by the side of the nearest pool. There are two kinds of relaxation.

I am rooming with Henry Hurley while we are here. Yes! At first I thought to myself 'What do I do?' I decided to break the ice and have a talk. Man to man! It is not my fault that I played in the three matches last week. He knew that, but he was still very disappointed. We had a good talk. We understand one another better now. This was to be a golden opportunity for him to win his first cap. He has trained very well all though the tour, and he has never avoided anything on the training field. All I could tell Henry is that his time will come. And I genuinely hope it will. He is a very strong player, but I want to stick around in a green jersey for a couple of more years.

The All Blacks are staying in another hotel in the complex, and so too are the Scottish girls! The Scottish Union flew them out here. It was a fine gesture, but I am glad the I.R.F.U. did not do that for our womenfolk. I would not want Rachel out in this country touring around, not unless I was close enough by her side. It is a dangerous place to be on your own. The I.R.F.U. have decided to give us travel vouchers worth £1,500 instead, which we can use at any time. That is a better idea, I think.

We also met some of the French boys, Morocco and Ondarts who are out here with a golden oldies team. We had a few drinks with them. Good fun. I also rang home this evening, and I was told that things have taken off in a fairly big way. The whole country is getting behind us. It is hardly like it was for Jack Charlton and the boys in the U.S. last year, but it is a change for us to be whipping up some real excitement. Hopefully we will have the country out dancing in the middle of the streets before this tournament is over.

Harry, who is one of our minders, told us today that a mate of his, who was guarding the All Blacks, was shot in the stomach outside his home on Sunday. He is supposed to be in pretty bad shape but it looks like he will recover.

TUESDAY, JUNE 6:

We left Sun City in the late afternoon, so most of us got up early to try and make the most of the time we had left. I set off with Noisy, Paddy Johns and Joe Doran. There was no transport we could find, but we gave a few bob to this coach driver to take us on a short, unofficial tour. We went straight to an alligator park, but they were all taking it easy, just basking in the sun and ignoring us. They could not have cared less about the four Micks shouting at them to move a little. We decided to throw a few branches at them, to offer them some encouragement, you know! But we got caught. Typical!

Noisy talked our way out of the spot of bother. He told the attendants, who were increasing in numbers by the second, that we were only trying to feed the poor creatures. I don't know whether they bought it or not, but they were still pretty thick-looking as we left.

Our next stop was an aviary. Joe Doran was very interested in the feathered birds, as it turns out, but I would have preferred looking at the naked types we almost caught a glimpse of in Johannesburg.

We were back in Pretoria this evening. We met up with Zinzan and Robin Brooke, and Lomu, and they were relaxed and talkative. Though it is easy to see they are on all systems go to win the whole thing.

WEDNESDAY, JUNE 7:

This morning, I went for yet another haircut with Halpin. Anything to escape the hotel and pass a couple of hours, though the only problem is we did not have much hair to begin with this morning. The two of us will have to think up some other way of passing the time if we are into the semi-finals next week.

There was a team meeting at midday and we trained after it. Very, very hot today! We were supposed to have a scrummaging session against the Scots, who are also staying around here somewhere, but that fell through. I am glad it did. I do not see much point in looking for too much extra work after the strain of last week. And I think it is a better idea to keep our distance from other teams when there is serious work to be done.

At tonight's meeting, we went through the French team with the help of George Spotswood who had portions of their matches broken into segments on the video for us. There was a very positive feeling all through the meeting. Everybody realises we are now entering unknown waters. We have already achieved the target we set ourselves in this tournament but tomorrow we pack for Durban and hopefully we have a lot of rugby still in front of us. All in all, it was another superb analysis by George. We know each other a long time now, and a lot of people think of him as George in the Union, but he is probably one of the best readers of the game in the country.

THURSDAY, JUNE 8:

The team for Saturday was announced this morning. Richie Wallace is out and Daragh O'Mahony is in. We all feel sorry for Richie. It is not nice for any player to be left out of things at this stage of the tournament. Having said that, O'Mahony got his first cap against Italy when he was carrying an injury, and he deserves another chance quickly enough. The second cap is always a good cap to win. The only pity is that his parents were over for the tournament last week, thinking he would play against Japan, and they have gone home now.

We arrived in Durban early this afternoon. It was another short, pleasant flight, but we are now in yet another Holiday Inn. Same walls, same curtains, same food! The good thing is that there is a big Irish contingent already in the hotel and they are in great form.

On the table-tennis front, Mr Popplewell and Mr. Geoghegan trounced Mr. Burke and Mr. Mullin, and I will not humiliate them further by announcing the score. The sweat flowed off me by the bucketful during the game. God knows what it will be like on the rugby pitch, where there will be no air-conditioning! We trained on the back pitch at King's Park, and there was a good breeze for most of the session. That helped, though there were a big number of people out watching us and it took some time for the sharpness to come into the work we were doing. From now on we will be having closed sessions. Just to keep out the Nosy Parkers from some other team.

Nearly everybody was narky on the field with one another, and that is a good sign. It tells us that everybody is concentrating on the match on Saturday.

Tonight I slipped out of the hotel with Noisy to a nice fish restaurant overlooking the beach. Before leaving we were told to be careful by the folks in the hotel. They told us that on the beachfront people can get mugged in a second. On the 'Golden Mile', which was an old whites-only strip of hotels and restaurants, there is very little wealth on view. It is now known as 'Muggers Mile'. Noel and I walked quickly from A to B.

Telephoned Rob Andrew tonight. Just to say hello, and ask him did he realise that Ireland had its name on the Webb Ellis Trophy?

FRIDAY, JUNE 9:

There is a super view from our bedroom windows in the hotel. Durban looks the most attractive place we have been in so far, but everybody has told us it is really dreary and dangerous. Anyhow, a couple of photographers wanted shots of a few Irish players casually walking along the beautiful beaches. How I hate these requests?

I was first man on the beach. 'Where's the cameras boys?' Terry also shows up, and we are supposed to walk up and down, and pretend to be deep in thought, looking at one another and looking out at the Indian ocean. All I did was splash some water at him, that's all I did! But, of course, he is the Irish captain and he has to end up soaking me. And me with my camera in my hand. It was not a fair fight. What a big bully Kingston is!

Guess who I went shopping with? Halpin and I sweated like two little pigs as we browsed around for an hour. Back in the lift in the hotel I met J.P.R. Williams. He wished us the best and thought we have a decent chance against France. Met up with Neil McCann from Fyffes in our hotel as well, and we had a cup of coffee together. He's a good supporter and he gets to most of our matches.

This afternoon we went to King's Park to have a good look around the place. The pitch is in absolutely beautiful condition. Perfect. We did 10 to 15 lineouts while we were there.

Every ground over here has a large souvenir shop, and it is hard to walk by them and ignore them. This is the sort of thing we should have at home. It is a quick and easy way of making money for clubs. As usual I buy a few things. Back in the hotel Geoghegan is dying with a dose which looks and sounds like the 'flu. There is no doubt but that he will be playing tomorrow however. Even if he had a broken leg he would be playing. Willie John McBride is around the place and he wishes us the best tomorrow.

Dinner this evening was followed by a movie which was total crap, and the name of which I honestly cannot even remember. I walked out of the cinema halfway through it with one or two of the boys. Good man Franno! He is never going to fill Barry Norman's shoes as a film critic for the B.B.C.

SATURDAY, JUNE 10:

It is probably just as well we lost today. I don't mean to throw my hat at the World Cup by saying that, but the way we lost suggested that we were close enough to being a spent force. It would be great to play South Africa in the semi-finals next weekend. It would probably be a fantastic experience, but I think we might be in big trouble in that sort of game. The mental relief of having reached the quarter-finals, which was always our goal, was obviously much bigger than any of us had realised.

We did not have it in us to really carry the game to the French like we did against the All Blacks and the Welsh. Our pack did not work like one unit. We were fragmented. The French were not much better than us in the first-half and they did not score their two tries until the very end of the match.

The scoreline, 36-12, suggests that they were three times as good as us, but that is not accurate. In the end they were twice as good perhaps, though they needed Thierry Lacroix kicking penalties like there was no tomorrow. He kicked eight, I'm told. And a lot of them were from difficult angles.

Saint-Andre scored their first try and then N'Tamack got their second after intercepting a pass from Brennie Mullin when we were inside their 22 metres line. Watching him running the length of the field to score, with Brennie chasing after him, was annoying. But it was all long over by then. That was just the icing on the cake for them. Though I don't think they really deserved it.

We deserved to lose, there's no doubt about that. We

were not hunting and foraging like we should have been, and like we said we would! The first-half was a strange sort of game. The French looked to be holding back slightly and their out-half Christophe Deylaud was making a mess of whatever good possession they won. We were holding back too. It was so warm out there on the pitch, and I think both teams were a little bit unsure of themselves.

We were level at half-time and they did not go in front until about 10 minutes into the second-half. Eric and Lacroix kicked four penalties each in the first-half, but there is no doubt they were winning most of the possession. Roumat and Merle in the middle of the lineout and especially Cabannes at the back got their hands on far too much ball. Fulcher won a fair bit of ball before he had to go off injured, but generally speaking Eric and Niall were not given a fair chance because of the French dominance.

It is hard to explain why we did not ruck and drive and maul like we did last week. We had the best of intentions. We wanted to get stuck into the French like we did against the All Blacks and the Welsh, but it just did not happen. I can not say why? This felt like one game too much in a short period of time. For months and months we had been thinking of New Zealand, Japan and Wales, and only those three teams. Switching onto the French and imagining this game as the most important game we might ever play in our lives was not easy. Last week it was easy to think that way!

Corkery and Bell looked the same players they were last week, but the rest of us did not. That's about it. To beat France and get to the semi-finals our pack had to be every bit as aggressive and tigerish as we had been up to now. It's a pity, even though nobody in the dressing room was heart-broken after the match. There was just a feeling of general disappointment. That says something too, I suppose.

We will never know what we missed by not qualifying for the semi-finals. To play South Africa in the semi-final of the World Cup would undoubtedly have been the greatest experience any of us would have had in our careers.

It is hard to imagine what that game would have been like. We will never know now. Everything felt good in the camp this morning. When Terry said his piece at the team meeting we all felt we were going to really test the French. We thought we would win. I met Ed Morrison before the match and he was in good form and talkative. There's no harm in talking to the ref!

The crowd in the stadium was small. The place only looked half full and there was none of the atmosphere we have had at our games up to now. Certainly it was nothing like Ellis Park last Sunday. It was sort of dead this time, and maybe that had an effect on the French and ourselves.

Though it suited them to play a dead game more than us. They were always capable of coming alive and taking the game on at any time. We realised that we needed to get into the game from the word go. It's all over now. No point in trying to look at it this way or that way! We lost. We have to go home.

Halpin and myself agreed to meet Willie John and J.P.R. in the pub around the corner from the stadium after the match, but we couldn't find them. We didn't stick around for too long. Tonight is going to be a long night. I imagine we will be giving it a reasonable lash out on the town. After the Welsh match, we had a few drinks, but apart from that it has been a long, hot, dry tour.

SUNDAY, JUNE 11:

We said good-bye to hot and humid Durban this morning. There were a lot of sore heads on the 'plane, which goes nicely with the damage we have picked up along the way during the World Cup. Fulcher has a cracked clavicle in his left shoulder from yesterday's game. Johns has an eye injury. Corkery messed up one of his ankles, and Eric did damage to his hand. Denis McBride has something like 20 stitches in his head since the Welsh match. We are the picture of health today.

The Bath under-15 team were on the 'plane to Johannesburg with us. Nice for 15 years-olds to tour South Africa! It goes to show what sort of development is going on in some English clubs right now.

Rob Andrew will be the new king of England for the rest of the year! His dropped goal in the final seconds beat Australia in the quarter-final in Cape Town. England are still on course and it is going to take an outstanding performance from somebody to stop them now. They play the All Blacks next weekend. That will be interesting to say the least.

I'm very happy for Rob. He is such a dedicated player, in addition to being a good boy to know off the pitch. They will be throwing the awards at him now. B.B.C. Sportstar of the Year! A Knighthood! He will get the lot probably. He deserves it.

We are in a Holiday Inn close to the airport tonight. We went to the Waterfront place, which was one of the first places we looked around at the start of the tournament, but this time we went there in search of all the alcohol we could find. Last time in the Waterfront it was water and lots of ice mostly.

We are retracing our steps, but everybody would prefer

to get home as quickly as possible. The World Cup is over for us now. There is no point hanging around here. There are things to be done at home. Things which have absolutely nothing to do with an oval ball, thank God!

MONDAY, JUNE 12:

We were up early this morning, only to discover that there was a cock-up about to happen. Behind the scenes during this tournament, there has been an awful lot of chaos. Even though the tournament is over for us and we just want to get home, the chaos was still following us.

We understood originally that we would be flying out tonight, but we were then told by South African Airways that we would not have a flight home until Thursday, or possibly even Friday. An extra three days out here was not what anybody wanted. There was probably not any alcohol left in the Waterfront for starters. As well as that, we were probably staying in the worst hotel in the whole of Africa.

Noisy, once more, came to the rescue and, within a couple of hours, he had us booked to fly out from Johannesburg on a different airline. He said that if the World Cup committee do not cover our costs then the I.R.F.U. will. The way Noel Murphy gets work done behind the scenes is often amazing. We flew out at 9.0 p.m. and everybody was relieved to be on our way.

There were only five or six first class seats available to us. I did not get one of them. The main thing on my mind is getting home, and I did not care too much about where I was to sit. I had the offer to stay out in South Africa with one of the supporters groups, but I am glad that I turned that idea down. It would simply be hard work.

During the flight, I slipped upstairs to first class and I

found myself some space. I slept for a few hours. Where there is a will to find room, there is room!

My Irish player of the World Cup is the same choice as everybody else's. It has to be David Corkery. He is an example to everybody involved in Irish rugby and especially young players who want to do something with their careers. After a good tour out in Australia last year and a bad game against England in the opening game of the championship, he was dropped from the team. Everybody was toilet against the English, not just Corkery.

He reacted by working himself hard and he has left nobody in any doubt in recent weeks but that he is someone who will lead the Irish team for many years to come. I was not on the Australian tour, so I did not know much about him 12 months ago. All I know is that he now has a physical presence which very few Irish backrow players in recent times have had. He is a phenomenal player.

Paddy Johns had a very good tournament as well. He came out here right after his first child had been born and, while he did not actually give birth himself, he was able to knuckle down and concentrate on the matches which had to be played. He never showed any sign of having his mind elsewhere.

Terry was the same rock he always is. Denis McBride fought to the last drop of his blood. Jonny Bell was superb. To completely do his finger in in one game and play on, and play bloody well! A lot of players did things during the last few weeks which shows that there is an amount of spirit and character in this Irish squad. I know we disappointed against the French, but it is important to look at the four games we played out here, and to look at the individual performances from some people! This was a good tournament from Ireland's point of view. We have shown that while we may have problems, we are capable of facing up to them in the near future. We can be a respectable rugby team. There is no doubt about that.

It is wrong to be picking out individual players now and praising them. This was one big, united effort and the pack proved that against the All Blacks and against the Welsh. We were there for one another and we were ready to take on anything.

I feel sorry for the players, like Staples and Woody, who had to leave the tournament halfway through. I feel a bit sorry for Simon Geoghegan as well. It was the usual story for him. He got very little ball with which to play around and run with. He would have loved to do so much more in this World Cup. He did very well. He brought off great tackles and by his presence on the field alone he gives great strength to the team.

It was a good tournament. The semi-finals have still to be played, but they look like serving up an appropriate ending to the tournament. My money is on the All Blacks. I would also like them to do it, that's if England don't do it!

We finished equal fifth in the world, and that sounds pretty good. We were never going to win the World Cup. The standard of rugby in the tournament continues to rise every four years, and some people thought we would not even be seen in South Africa this time! Well, the world saw us and even though we did not set the place alight with the quality of our play at times, I am sure we still had our admirers and made lots of new friends in other countries.

We can still survive. I suppose that is the message we bring home from this World Cup. We can still survive against the best teams. But it would be nice to some day think of beating the likes of Australia and the All Blacks.

Surviving against them is okay, but it is no fun and in the long run it can only be demoralising for the game at home.

For the next World Cup, in four years time, it is vital that Ireland becomes one of the serious players. We have to become far more determined about what we are doing. Rugby is now a serious business.

CHAPTER 11

ALL BLACKS AND ME!

I watched the 1995 World Cup final between South Africa and New Zealand in Simon Geoghegan's home in London. Neil Francis was also there, and the three of us were completely absorbed by the occasion and, most especially, by the match itself. My colours were pinned to the All Blacks' mast. They were my team.

Sean Fitzpatrick and his boys lost a fantastic match. I was genuinely sorry for them because I thought they had proved without any shadow of a doubt over the previous five weeks of the tournament that they were the best team in the world. On the day of the final, they faced a Springbok team which had an enormous amount of passion and emotion on their side. It was 15 New Zealanders against all of South Africa! It also did not help Sean Fitz very much to have 11 of his players go down with food poisoning in the 24 hours before the match.

Possibly, at the end of the day, the All Blacks depended far too much for their own good on Jonah Lomu. The winger was 18 stones, six feet and five inches tall at the beginning of the tournament and he just grew and grew.

Initially, Lomu was unstoppable, but South Africa did their sums the week before the final and they came up with the right answers. They opened spaces to allow him to run at them and then they usually had three people covering that space. It might have been wiser if Lomu was used as more of a decoy against the Springboks. Then again, it is easy to be wise after the event. Imagine having Jonah Lomu in your team and deciding not to give him much of the ball?

The coach who ever came up with that strategy might be in danger of being locked up. In Ireland, we stand accused of ignoring Simon Geoghegan most of the time but I can assure you it is not a conscious decision on anybody's part. Our trouble is winning good, fast ball first of all, and then getting it out to Simon!

Talking to Sean Fitz, after we had played New Zealand in our opening game in the World Cup, he explained to me their predicament with regard to Lomu. The left winger had not figured in their planning at all in the run-up to the tournament. It was the national sevens competition in New Zealand which suddenly unveiled this man the size of a lock forward who could sprint with anybody. Lomu had only been a reserve at the All Blacks trial a little while before that.

'What do you do?' asked Sean Fitz? The All Blacks are normally a complete, 15-man side but all of a sudden they had this giant on the wing with the number 11 shaved out of one of his eyebrows. They found themselves shipping too much ball out to him. It worked to the team's advantage in the semi-final against England when Lomu scored four tries, but it was not going to work forever.

We had heard more than enough about Jonah Lomu before our defeat by the All Blacks, but we did not take that much notice of him. When you are playing the All Blacks you are playing the All Blacks! There is nobody you can ignore.

We did not worry greatly about Lomu and Lomu alone. Seeing him run with such speed and break through tackles with such ease in that first game left us stunned. His powerful run the length of the field in the second-half when he brushed off or skipped by four tacklers before being halted by Geoghegan was unbelievable. On that occasion, he finished off his performance by tipping the ball up for Kronfeld to score.

It has got to be said, however, that if one man can get a hold of him then most other players should be able to do the same. If you get close enough and get down low enough, then Lomu will fall. Simon Geoghegan is a fiercely tenacious player admittedly and that's what is needed most of all against Lomu, in my opinion - the will to get him down! Just looking at him can convince many players that the man is beyond them. They have to get up close to him to be successful.

South Africa, in the final, also made sure that the ball which was sent in his direction was slow ball. Lomu was not allowed to build up any great speed at any stage in the match. And when he got the ball, somebody was on him immediately.

All this Jonah Lomu talk, however, does a great disservice to the All Blacks as a team. They have always been a fantastic team. The best team there has ever been in rugby union! Team is the important word.

The All Blacks are the Brazil of rugby. The South Americans have always ruled one brand of football. The All

Blacks rule another, and it is one of the greatest honours any player can achieve just to play against them.

It is an honour which I have had 10 times. I do not know whether that is some sort of record for an Irish player or not. It is not something I have ever checked out or queried. For Leinster and Ireland, the Baa-baas and the Lions I have experienced the magic of the All Blacks and whether I am some class of record holder or not, I do consider myself to be one of the luckiest Irish rugby players of all time.

I was only a child (of 25 years of age) when I first played against them during their tour of Wales and Ireland back in 1989. That was Wayne Shelford's team, and Alex Wyllie was coach. They had won the first World Cup tournament two years earlier. John Gallagher was full-back. John Kirwan was badly injured by the time they flew into Ireland, but they had Grant Fox, Richard Loe, the Whetton brothers, Mike Brewer and a galaxy of big names.

Awesome is not a word I particularly like because of the frequency of its use, but to me it is a word which was created especially to fit the All Blacks. Virtually any New Zealand team! In the last six years, as I keep bumping into them, I have made friends with about half a dozen of them and I have discovered that they are, in fact, human beings. Once you put faces on them and do not see them dressed all in black, they become another team at the bar. A great and fantastic team, but another rugby team nevertheless.

Olo Brown, their tight head prop, I now consider a good friend. Sean Fitz is a good boy too. I get on the 'phone to them or go on the piss with them or one or two others, and while I respect them the same way as I respected them that first day back in 1989, I no longer fear them.

The Haka, I now quite enjoy to be honest. It looks an intimidating piece of work, and it sounds bloody fearsome, but it is really only a party-piece. Usually, I just want them to get on with it and get on with the game.

It is important to face the Haka as a mark of respect and, also, by looking them in the eye the All Blacks attain less of a psychological advantage with their ranting and raving. Besides there are always three or four members of their team who have very little idea of what they are supposed to be doing. It can be quite funny actually. I now tell younger or inexperienced teammates of mine to pick out an All Black who clearly looks to be in trouble as soon as the Haka commences.

Sure enough, there is always at least one of their number who is totally out of sync with everybody else. It is a bit like when other players try to sing their National anthems before a match. They have all heard the song a million times, but a lot of players are soon lost for words.

I have indeed been lucky to play against them so often. In most rugby careers players might only get three or four matches against the All Blacks, and they might only tour the country once. I have had two tours out there. At the end of the Lions trip in 1993 I had the opportunity of staying in Auckland to play for a few months, but I was too tired. I had two years of non-stop rugby behind me and a 13-match tour! It was a pity I had to decline the offer. I would have loved it, I'm sure.

In the 10 matches I have played I can not remember one which was not brutally hard. I would probably rate seven or eight of those matches in the 10 most memorable matches of my career to date. Their scrummaging unit is always tops! Australia and South Africa would come after them in my book in that department, and England and France further behind. With New Zealand, from scrum one to scrum 21, it is bang, bang, BANG! There is no let-up, no holding anything back.

In the World Cup this time, the All Blacks as a team were not the finished article. Half a dozen of their key players were only starting out on their careers. And still, they almost won the damn thing!

I wanted them to do it, not only because I like them, but also because I was not all that fond of the South Africans. I look at and listen to Louis Luyt, president of the South African union, and it is obvious that they considered themselves the best in the world anyhow. They probably did not need to win the World Cup to make that official in their own eyes.

I would love to see this present South African team now go to New Zealand and see can they win a series down there! At the end of that, we would then know their true standing in the world.

No team can afford to insult the All Blacks, and Sean Fitz and his boys were clearly insulted by some of the things which were said after the World Cup final. Before the semi-finals, I read a quote from somebody in the English squad saying they thought they would have the edge over New Zealand in the scrum. It was not an insult, but it was a very silly thing to say. It is crazy for any team to imagine themselves having a natural advantage over the All Blacks in any sector. The South African pack did better in the final than England did, but the South African boys were getting away with a lot of messing in my view and the referee was not dealing with them appropriately.

The All Blacks' great secret, it appears to me, is that they do not make mistakes. They do not hand over the ball to the opposition. Traditionally, they have always played it simple and with the minimum of risk by putting the ball into the opposition half. Conceding handy penalties is not in their nature and is not part of their game plan.

In the World Cup that same logic was the centrepiece of their performance, but coach Laurie Mains also saw to it that his team moved the ball faster than ever before. Rucks led to lightning fast ball for out-half Andrew Mehrtens and, with his speed and the speed around him, it was natural and easy enough for them to throw the ball around more than ever before and run from deeper positions.

The All Blacks, in South Africa, showed us their old game and a whole new game in five short weeks. It was not quite revolutionary. The same old pressure which they always apply in matches was there the same as before. Sean Fitz would start shouting 'Quicken it up! QUICKEN IT UP!' whenever he thought the opposing team was in trouble.

And, sure enough, for five or six minutes the All Blacks would go into over-drive, swinging the ball wide, left and right, searching for that weakness in the opposing defence, and finding it!

This time, the All Blacks were a lighter side than ever before and Mains said many times during the tournament that they purposely chose the squad on the smaller side. They did not have many big lumps of men on the pitch, even though their front row was huge as usual. Ian Jones is not that big in the second row. He is only about 16 stones, and Robin Brooke is only reasonably big. Kronfeld is relatively small. But Mains knew what he was doing obviously. The grand design of the New Zealand coach was to match the opposition for power and run them off the pitch at the same time. It almost worked perfectly.

I have never seen a rugby match played with the intensity of the World Cup final. It was rivetting, right from the first glimpse of Nelson Mandela wearing Francois Pienaar's Springbok jersey.

Imagine John Major wearing Will Carling's jersey in the middle of Twickenham? Imagine Mary Robinson out on Lansdowne Road in Terry Kingston's number two? I don't think Terry's jersey would quite fit our President.

Mandela, besides being a fantastic leader, is a very real human being. He has power, charm, humility, and he also seems to have the utter respect of most of the whites in South Africa which is terrific to see. Mandela was able to carry off the trick of wearing Pienaar's jersey, and that's what it was, a political trick as much as anything else! The leader of the country and the Springbok captain are reported to be friends but, by wearing the jersey, Mandela was also engaging himself in the process of uniting the country. Fair dues to him.

There was a huge amount of emotion in evidence before the game began, but I have to admit that I was not all that moved by it. It looked to me as though the South Africans were full of themselves as usual and were behaving as though they already had the Webb Ellis trophy locked away in their cabinet. The New Zealanders can be an arrogant lot as well, I know that, but at the present time in world rugby they had every right to be. The Springboks did not have that right during the World Cup.

Over there, Francois Pienaar was God. And that was before he got the country to the World Cup final and before South Africa won it! Winning was worth an awful lot of money to the Springbok captain and his team. Now they are nearly all like Gods in the eyes of their people. The pity is that there is only one black God amongst them, but the South African union are reportedly doing a lot of work on that front and they have promised more blacks and coloureds on their teams in the near future.

Pienaar is a good player and an honest player. I have only spoken to him on a couple of occasions and he seems a good boy, even though it is hard to know what some of the South Africans are really thinking. Pienaar has cleaned up the team's image in the last couple of years and he has completed a remarkable turnaround on the P.R. front.

On the field, during the World Cup, he often lived offside and if he was not captain of South Africa, I am pretty sure referees would have noticed him more. He is not the quickest wing forward in the world, but he does a lot of hard grafting and he always plays his heart out.

Everything on the day of the final was loaded against New Zealand. I felt sorry for them, even though in many respects it was a case of them getting a dose of their own medicine. In New Zealand, they are not adverse themselves to loading the odd match against touring teams, and taking full advantage of the crowd and the atmosphere, and the referee.

In the next few years, it might be battle after battle between New Zealand and South Africa. The Springboks will undoubtedly further improve, just as they have progressed over the last two or three years when they moved from the wilderness to become world champions.

Seeing England end up in a bit of a heap at the end of the World Cup was a pity. I genuinely mean that! They were blown off the pitch by the All Blacks and they lost for the first time in years to France in the play-off for third place.

Richards, Clarke and Rodber were the biggest back row in the tournament and they had the ability to take on and beat the All Blacks in a more traditional type of game. The three of them have the ability to control so much ball! And normally they can spoil the opposition and slow down the pace of the game sufficiently. But against the All Blacks the game by-passed them.

The first-half 25 points blitz was the result of total rugby from Sean Fitz and his team. The game was played at a level which England had not even reached. Right from the kick-off, with the English forwards lined up and anticipating the conventional start, the All Blacks announced that the match was not going to be an old-fashioned forward battle. When Mehrtens switched the kick-off to the left instead, where Lomu was waiting to pressurise the English defence, Jack Rowell's great game plan was in big trouble.

When Mehrtens got the ball in his hands for the first time in the match, instead of lofting the ball high to test Mike Catt, he threw a long pass! England had prepared impeccably for the World Cup for almost two years, but they were not prepared for the game which the opposition decided to play in the semi-final. Mains had neatly side-stepped his opposite number and left Rowell for dead on the sideline.

I felt sorry for the English boys and Will Carling. I admire Will. He has taken a great deal of flak over the years from people who do not know too much about rugby and he has gone through some rough patches with his own form, but he has always come out on the other side and remained strong.

The deep respect which the English players have for him was evidenced before the World Cup when he put his foot in it by calling the English rugby union a bunch of old farts. Richards and Andrew would not even consider taking up the captaincy once Will had been stripped of it, and the rest of the players united behind their former captain like a tight family.

Over the years, Will has certainly done his own thing and prospered personally. Publicity is a big part of his business and promoting Will Carling is one of his goals. But he has never let his team down and he has never put himself before the team when it has mattered.

The Carling years appeared to come to an abrupt halt in South Africa, but it would be very wrong to label them a failure of any description. England beat the All Blacks, South Africa and Australia in recent years and any team which collects those three scalps deserves to go down in history as one of the greatest teams of all time.

After beating Australia in their quarter-final, England found it hard to turn around and take on the All Blacks a week later. There was very little room left for any improvement in those seven days. It was a situation which was similar in many ways to that encountered by the majority of the English players when they were playing for the Lions in 1993. Then, we had beaten the All Blacks in the second test with a fantastic performance, and we had to do it all over again seven days later! The Lions were unable to do it. England came aground in South Africa on that same psychological rock as much as anything else.

It is hard for an Irishman to criticise England or feel sorry for them for too long! To me the standard of their club rugby is brilliant, for instance, and yet I hear them complaining about the poor level of competition. The same way we hear, in Ireland, that the All Ireland League is only of mediocre standard. Our club system is streets behind theirs, but they want to improve theirs even further! It is really a frightening thought. Where does it leave us when the top clubs in England are dreaming of reaching the same standard as Queensland and Transvaal?

The game in England will further improve. Rowell, for example, will have learned his lesson in 1995. The English players in future will be on playing contracts and the gap between them and the southern hemisphere countries will be narrowed. There is no doubt about that.

Again, where does it leave us? Look how England have advanced in the last decade? Geoff Cooke's squad won two grand slams, but that regime already looks old hat. England do not care it seems about the recent past. They are ploughing forward, and the day when the player in England trains, eats, sleeps and plays rugby, and does nothing else, is at hand.

England will put the 1995 World Cup behind them and get on with a new and better way of playing rugby. When they dismally kicked their way to defeat against France in the last game of the tournament, some commentators were prepared to write off Rowell and Carling and the boys, but those people are badly wrong in their judgement. England obviously did not care about third and fourth place. They travelled out to South Africa to win the World Cup, and nothing less!

England had done everything they thought they needed to do in advance of the tournament. The physical, mental and dietary requirements of the squad were fully met, everything down to purchasing full-length and hooded rubber suits to help with the squad's acclimatisation needs. The suits were made especially for each player and cost something like £500 each! They were developed by the navy to help against hypothermia in life or death situations. Rowell's team used them in preparation for life or death situations on the hot rugby fields of South Africa.

The English team died at the end of the World Cup, but not for long! Australia probably have bigger problems to face up to in the near future than England. Michael Lynagh is now gone, and Campese appears to be very close to the end of his dramatic career. Australia suffered two tough defeats in South Africa. England encountered one hard defeat, and an unimportant defeat by France.

Rugby union has come to the surface in Australia in the last decade. The game is now packaged very well, and young kids are being enticed away from more popular sports like cricket and Australian Rules football. Bob Dwyer is largely responsible for that. He created the team which won the World Cup in 1991, but he obviously found it hard to maintain that impetus.

Great coaches, the same as great players, cannot go on forever. In the last couple of years, Campo was turning a match on its head once in every three games rather than every second game. He always put his money where his mouth was and you would have to admire him for his style and panache, but in South Africa he stepped into the future with a pair of old legs under him.

The unluckiest team in the whole tournament was probably France, our quarter-final conquerors. They timed their performances exactly right and got better and better as the weeks passed. Even allowing for a dreadful out-half, they should have beaten the Springboks in the semi-final.

The French were right there at the end of the match, and they had South Africa beaten! They deserved a late try to win the game. The home team were out on their feet. Pienaar and the boys were gone, but time saved them.

Whatever advancements are made in world rugby, the French will always be able to match any other team. They will always be overly-casual one minute and incredibly exciting the next minute. It is not in their nature to take out a blackboard and sit in front of it, like the All Blacks! That is the beauty and the greatness of French rugby, their complete and utter unpredictability.

If the type of game which the All Blacks unveiled in South Africa is to be the future of rugby, then the French will be happy enough. Doing everything fast and throwing the ball about all over the place, with forwards and backs switching roles, will suit the French more than any other country.

All we know for sure is that rugby union will never again be pedestrian. Forwards are going to have to behave and play like backs, and backs might have to look like Jonah Lomu! The great memory of the World Cup is one of Jonah Lomu's runs against England. Tony Underwood bounced off him, Dean Richards and Tim Rodber fell under his feet, and Martin Johnson and Victor Ubogu went for a ride on his back. A left winger doing the work of almost an entire pack! Unbelievable! But we did witness it in South Africa.

The All Blacks are the team we remember most from the 1995 World Cup finals. The Springboks are second in that regard. The style and speed and sheer adventure of the All Blacks' play set an agenda which every other team in the world now has to consider.

Our old fashioned ways in the Five Nations championship will hardly get us very far in the future. The championship is admittedly a fantastic show. It attracts full houses at every single game and ignites fierce passion. But the question now has to be asked: are we fooling ourselves by getting over-excited by the Five Nations?

Without being disrespectful towards us, the All Blacks

and their neighbours in the southern hemisphere have probably thought so for a long time.

CHAPTER 12

THE CAPTAINS AND THE KINGS

The fact that I captained Ireland for no more than 20 minutes in my career to date is of no great regret to me, though having said that, I would not have minded seeing out the entire game against Japan in last Summer's World Cup finals. As soon as Terry Kingston replaced Keith Wood in that game I assumed Terry would also take over his old job as well. I had no problem in letting him take charge. He was excellent in that role throughout the tour. The best man for the job!

It honestly does not bother me whether I am ever again chosen as the best man to lead Ireland out onto the field. It is a great honour to captain your country and, naturally, I would not turn it down if I was ever asked again, but it is also a job which brings with it huge responsibilities.

And it so happens that, in rugby, the hooker or somebody in the backrow is in the best position to carry out those responsibilities.

I honestly feel that with my personal sort of game I can probably do more leading on the field when I am NOT captain, if you understand? I can get more involved vocally in my own way and in my own time, and I feel that my general performance is a help to the team captain. When I am captain, I feel slightly restricted. The hooker or the back row forward has greater opportunity to be on top of the play than a prop.

Having said that, captaining Ireland once (even for 20 minutes) was enjoyable and satisfying. Nowadays in rugby, with the way the media run around after the captain, there can be a fair amount of glory going with the job, but that is no reason to want to do it. A good captain must feel capable of imposing himself on his team when things are going wrong and he must feel capable of making the right decisions at the crucial moments in every game. And he should feel sure that his team's chances of winning can be greatly improved by the quality of his decision-making.

It is a big, difficult job! An awful lot depends on the individual in question. Some people can take the captaincy thing in their stride, whereas some other people will find themselves stumbling underneath the extra weight.

Will Carling is the classic captain in the modern game. He is cool, composed and very much at home leading England. He has made the job of England rugby captain equal, in terms of importance and prestige, to the job of the England cricket captain and the hype and the pressures seldom seem to get through to him. He still gets his job done in the centre for England, in addition to making the right decisions and encouraging those around him. Will Carling, of course, has been blamed by some people for making himself larger than life, and possibly larger than the entire English team! If that was the case, it was hardly Will's fault.

Because he fits the bill as English captain almost perfectly, the British media has put a lot of work into building him up into a national figure. Is he to blame for that? Hardly. In the English camp he is thoroughly respected by all the players, even after all these years, and there is certainly no streak of envy visible within his squad.

In Ireland, the team captain will never get the same attention as Will Carling. Our captain has to stand up and say his bit after matches, and journalists will consistently run to him between matches, but the likes of Mullin or Geoghegean or Bell will always get as much attention as the Irish captain. Possibly when we win two or three grand slams on-the-trot that will change!

If Simon Geoghegan ever becomes captain of Ireland, no other player might ever get a look in, such is the interest he already attracts, though somehow I can never see Simon looking for the job. He is not that type of guy. Simon is his own man and a fantastic support to all the other players, but he will always be an original. No, I doubt if he will ever lead Ireland onto the field at Lansdowne Road. Anyhow,the rest of us would probably be half a mile behind him.

A good hooker will make a better captain that a great winger any day of the week. If a forward is needed to captain a team, then the hooker is the first man who is always looked at. For starters, he has the key role in the lineout. He is in the best position to see exactly what is happening and what his own players are up to, or not up to, whichever is the case.

A back row forward is also loose around the field and is expected to be in an ideal position to see what exactly is happening and what might be on. Meanwhile, the props or the second row are most likely buried somewhere most of the time. Physically, too, we are not designed to be flying around the field.

The Scottish teams of recent years had David Sole, Finlay Calder and Gavin Hastings as captain. A prop, a wing forward and a full-back, and Sole was every bit as successful as the other two, if not more so. It so happened, at the time, that Sole was the most inspirational character on the Scottish team. He led by example, and since he was a little on the light side, he was able to cover more ground than the average prop. Scrummaging, actually, was not the strongest part of David Sole's game.

In recent years, since the Ciaran Fitzgerald days, we have had Donal Lenihan, Willie Anderson, Rob Saunders, Philip Matthews, Mick Bradley, Brendan Mullin and Terry captaining the team, and two of them were from the second row! It happened that Lenihan was the most experienced player on the team after Fitzy retired and he was well respected by all the players. Anderson, on the other hand, was somebody who was a born leader of men and he was very much in the Fitzy mould as captain, though I must say that Fitzy still stands heads and shoulders above all the other captains.

I have to admit that I was always in awe of him. I would have loved to have had the opportunity to be in his dressing room when he was a player. It turned out that he was coaching Ireland when I finally got the chance to nail down my position in the front row and I found that Fitzy always got the very last ounce of energy and commitment out of every player in his company. He was unfortunate that Ireland's results in the early 90s did not match his performance as coach, but he came in at a time when the national team was in a bit of a hole.

It was no coincidence or fluke that Ireland came within a couple of minutes of defeating eventual World Cup champions, Australia during his reign. Fitzy was always capable of talking an Irish team into meeting any challenge head on.

When he captained the Lions in New Zealand in 1983, 10 years before I made my Lions debut in the same part of the world, Fitzy was torn asunder by some sections of the British media. That experience might have been the end for most players. The team, after all, lost all four test matches, but Fitzy bounced back two years later and proved something to his detractors when he led Ireland to a second Triple Crown. That demonstrated his strength as a player and as a human being.

Very few captains are so honoured because of their name or their performance. Leadership qualities usually blossom within a team. Terry Kingston is made of the same sort of stuff as Fitzy and in the present Irish team he is a natural choice as captain. He nearly always gets the mood in the dressing room exactly right, and with him around everybody finds it that bit easier to focus on the game at hand.

Terry led Ireland to the quarter-finals of the World Cup in South Africa, the same as Donal Lenihan did in 1987, and Philip Matthews in 1991. Who was the best Irish captain out of the three? That is a question which can not be factually answered.

Lenihan was not as loud or animated as most Irish captains. He was certainly no Willie Anderson, but he did things in his own quiet way. Anderson was 100% more vocal. Willie was the first Irish captain I played with, and he had a very positive and uplifting effect on players but perhaps, at times, he lifted the Irish team up a little bit too high!

It is important to get the balance just right with a team, not too relaxed, and not too focussed! Personally, for instance, I prefer a quieter approach to a match. Shouting in the dressing room has never done very much for me at any time in my career. I like to do my own thing in the last couple of hours before the kick-off and I like to turn myself on mentally at my own speed. I like to sit quietly and slowly gather together my own thoughts on the match and what I have to do on the pitch.

The last thing I need is to have somebody grabbing me and throwing me against a wall or banging heads. Geoghegan is always doing something like that with me in the Irish dressing room, and I hate it! He is just so wound up all the time and he is into the game long before he ever leaves the dressing room.

In the 90 minutes or so which a team spends in the stadium before a match, it is important for the captain to structure the time. Nobody wants to be standing around for too long. Likewise, very few people wish to be doing press-ups in the dressing room seconds before running onto the field. Only Simon perhaps.

The coach has backed out of the picture by then and the captain is at the controls. The team is in his hands, which is the way it should always be because the coach is not going to be around when you have the first ruck or line-out. The coach is usually hanging around when the team arrives into the dressing room upon arrival at the stadium and he pops his head in 40 minutes or so before the kick-off, but that is about all that needs to be seen of him. His work is over by that stage.

Philip Matthews was quieter than Willie Anderson, naturally enough, and he said what he had to say and then he usually said a whole lot more on the field through his fiercely committed play. I always enjoyed playing on teams captained by Philip, and I have to admit that I respected him more than any other captain I have ever played under in my whole career. He was such a superb player as well as a great captain.

Matthews and the Irish team went through some difficult years together and he shipped a fair amount of criticism from some quarters by the end of his International career. But in my mind he was always being picked out unfairly. It was a question of the captain being the easiest target for journalists who had no idea what else they could write about. Things were bad!

Like Fitzy, at times, Mick Bradley had to listen to a lot of people discussing whether he was on the team as a player or as a captain? It is really a silly question and arguing that point about Fitzy or Brad does both players a big injustice. Any fool could see they were both superb players most of the time, and no player is superb all the time! In their time, they played very well and they also captained Irish teams very well. Fitzy did so brilliantly.

Brad is Ireland's most capped scrum-half, so he must have been okay! With or without the captaincy! When he came back from the brink of retirement to succeed Matthews, he knew he would be walking into a bit of a storm. His father-in-law was manager of the team, after all, but anybody who knows Noel Murphy and anybody who knows Mick Bradley knows full well that Ireland will always come first with the pair of them, way ahead of family business.

The way it was, Ireland needed somebody experienced and with a sound head to settle things down and take charge of affairs. Brad might have found it more difficult late in his career to regain his place on the national team if the captaincy was also not there to be taken upon himself, but the two jobs went hand-in-hand. He was the right man for Ireland at the time, and nobody should ever have had any doubt about that.

When Rob Saunders came into the Irish team, in Fitzy's first year as coach, as scrum-half and captain, it did appear that the door was closed on Mick Bradley. But it was lucky for Ireland that he did not retire from the representative scene back in 1991 or '92. Saunders had plenty of enthusiasm and confidence, but it was hard on him being asked to captain his country when he was still virtually a kid and totally inexperienced.

He coped quite well, and better than most men his age would have had, but the pressures on him were huge and the media attention was something he did not need when he was also starting out on his career as an International scrum-half. His International career has since come to a standstill and, in my opinion, it might have been better for him personally if he had never been handed the captaincy.

Will Carling, admittedly, was also a young, relatively inexperienced player when he was asked to lead England back at the close of the 1980s. Someone like Saunders or Carling is always going to find it difficult initially to grasp the attention of everybody in the dressing room. It is tough for a 20 or 21 years-old to deal with a bunch of men in and around 30 years of age, especially when most of them think that they have heard it all and done it all before.

That must have been very hard on both of them, simply getting people to react to them! I found that when I captained Ireland against Japan(and I was 31 years old!) that there were two or three people in the dressing room whom I spoke to and got nothing back in return. It was as obvious as day. They were not prepared to accept me as captain overnight. I would have needed more time to get them on my side.

A young captain is probably going to meet with half a

dozen blank faces in his own dressing room straight off. That's the way it is. It can take time for a captain to be accepted by an entire team, because we're talking about 14 other individuals, don't forget.

Sonny Kenny, in Greystones, was the first captain I had who really inspired me. He was a hard customer in the pack. He looked after me, and I responded by doing whatever he told me to do. Tony Doyle was a good captain for Greystones, and so too were Johnny Murphy and Spud Murphy. They played with all their heart in every single game, and if a captain does that he will soon win over every player on his team.

I never captained Greystones myself, even though I was there for almost a decade. They wouldn't have me! Truthfully, it was a job I never went for. If I had stayed with the club I would like to think I would have been captain someday and I know I would have enjoyed it.

It is important that a captain is perfectly happy in his role. That brings us back to Will Carling again. He is probably the most celebrated rugby captain in this part of the world and at times it is like he was born into the role. It's him! The captaincy is him.

On the Lions tour to New Zealand in 1993, if Carling had been captain instead of Gavin Hastings, then he might not have lost his form on tour. His confidence might never have dipped. Not being captain might have had an effect on his performance. Who knows?

I have been on teams captained by Carling on a few occasions, and he is very, very good! He knows what to say. And he knows which players not to say very much to. He reads his role perfectly, and he never looks slightly flustered or excited by his extra duties. Because he is a total professional on and off the field, other players respect him, and they know he is utterly serious about what he is doing.

If anything, I found Carling to be quieter in the dressing room than I had first expected. We see so much of him and hear so much about him, and it is easy to expect somebody larger than life to walk though the door and start giving orders.

He has never said very much to me personally. Two or three words, and that's been about it! That's all I need to hear from him, and he knows it. With that I am ready to follow him onto the field and play my heart out. He obviously knows that is all I need to hear from him. Some players need a kick up the arse before a match and others need to be left alone. I am not the kickable kind.

Carling, Gavin Hastings, Sean Fitzpatrick, Nick Farr-Jones and Francois Pienaar have been the great captains in world rugby in my time. Though, to be honest, I doubt if any of them would have matched Ciaran Fitzgerald when it comes to calmly counting down the last few minutes before running out onto the field, and at the same time stoking the fire in the belly of the team.

I am happy to say that Fitzy was probably the greatest! It's strange, though, he led Ireland to two Triple Crowns and yet people do not speak of him as being a great hooker. They just speak of him as being a great captain. That is unfair.

Not all the captains I have just mentioned pop up in conversation when the Kings of the game are discussed. Will Carling, for all his ability and incredible success, will probably never be known as one of the great centres in world rugby. Farr-Jones was a great captain and a great scrum-half. Sean Fitz is equally impressive in both roles, though Pienaar, after the emotional ending to the World

Cup this last Summer, may never be known as an outstanding flanker.

The King of rugby union at present, if we believe what we saw in South Africa a few months ago, is that little boy by the name of Jonah Lomu. He inherited the title in South Africa from Campo. Lomu arrived as David Campese exited the International stage, it appears, and there were very few people who felt a great deal of sympathy for the brilliant Australian winger. Campo won more hearts on the field than he did off it.

It is wrong, in my mind, selecting individual players from the great teams in rugby and throwing vast amounts of praise at them as individuals. It is wrong, for instance, that 14 New Zealand players were over-shadowed in South Africa by one man on the left wing. No team is about just one player.

We can go through the All Blacks team which won the first World Cup in 1987, and we remember Buck Shelford, John Kirwan, Grant Fox and others. Who was the greatest player on that team? I would not be prepared to stick my neck out and give a personal answer. Kirwan won most praise in the newspapers, but Fox won most matches for the All Blacks on the field with his superb kicking.

The Australian team which won the World Cup over here in 1991 had an endless list of fantastic players as well, Farr-Jones, Lynagh, Willie O, Little, Horan, Eales! All great players. And each player a King in his own position. That is possibly the only way to fairly judge players, by looking at positions.

But is it right to pick out a scrum-half, like Farr-Jones for instance, without talking about his partnership and his brilliant relationship with Lynagh? They were a fantastic half-back pairing in my memory. I do not like seperating them now. They were superb together. A team within a team.

The same as a pack is a team within a team. With the English team, this Summer, it was the back row which won most praise. Rodber, Richards and Clarke are three remarkable players. Each commands his position, but put them together and they become even more impressive.

We can pick out individual players all the time, men like Blanco or Sella, but each was outstanding in a particular team and at a particular time. They entertained all on their own, as French players so often do, but lots of very good players on the field in blue and white helped, in big and small ways, to make it possible for them to be the players they were.

Lomu is King right now, but he has an awful lot of people to thank before he thinks of getting carried away with himself.

CHAPTER 13

IRELAND'S BALL?

God only knows where rugby union is going? And God only knows whether the game will prosper in years to come. The move from amateurism to professionalism is definitely going to be a quite traumatic change. The man who first listed death, divorce and moving house as the three awful changes in a person's life forgot to include the jump from amateurism to professionalism! Whether this move will be good or bad for the old game remains to be seen.

In the meantime, whatever about the health of the game itself, rugby players are about to prosper in a way which, five or ten years ago, most of us never even dreamed. There is no doubt but that money will help the game's best players. It should help the best players in every single country to become even better players. It will help reduce the pressures which have been building up on the International player in recent years as he found it increasingly difficult to balance his rugby career and his career outside the game. It will help enormously with families and dependants because, at least, all the time which the game consumes will be measured by monetary reward and will not just be all about the honour and glory of playing for your country.

The good thing is that the honour and glory can remain intact. All that needs to be added are some fat cheques!

This day was unavoidable.

Tennis, golf, athletics and practically every other sport known to man arrived at this exact point long before rugby union. Has professionalism damaged them or caused them any harm whatsoever? I don't think so. Millions of people still play tennis and golf just for the fun of it. People will continue to play rugby just for the fun of it as well, and having a professional side to the sport merely adds a new and unavoidable dimension.

I honestly do not feel there is any need for people in the game to worry unduly or fret over rugby's soul. There are exciting times ahead.

Once the World Cup in South Africa had ended, the Rugby Football Union in England had no option but to immediately hand contracts to its players. And once England did that it became imperative for Ireland, Scotland and Wales to look down the road towards semi-professionalism, and follow suit.

Throughout the 12 months leading up to the World Cup there had been constant talk about contracts and, in England, that talk was about both national contracts and club contracts. Obviously, in Ireland, where the numbers playing the game and supporting the game are so much smaller, there will never be a question of clubs being able to pay large numbers of the players on their books. But in England, the top clubs have the means to offer their top players suitable rewards for their time and effort. The club scene in England has always been far more professional in its organisation and approach than Ireland.

If contracts had not been made up and handed to the star players in the Five Nations, then it is quite likely that individuals would have been lost to a professional circus, like the one Kerry Packer had in mind and attempted to organise at the end of last Summer. Packer sought a new world league with 900 of the world's top players earning six-figure sums. If the Home Unions did not budge then the Five Nations' most precious assets would have started to go missing.

The English players, in the 1994-95 season for instance, reportedly earned sums in or around £16,000 each for their promotional work. Now they will earn £40,000 this season. It is a decent jump but, when you look at the work they put into the game and the money they help stuff into the pockets of the R.F.U., there is little doubt but that they are worth every penny of that.

Irish players, and the Welsh and Scots naturally, will always be worth less because we are less successful and face fewer pressures - but we are still worth something.

I have to admit that I was excited by the talk of the Packer deal. To receive a six-figure sum for playing the game I have always loved playing would have been like a dream. Although I had started a new career in London as a broker 12 months earlier, and that was vitally important to me, I was still impressed and attracted by the figures being reported in the newspapers.

The Irish players, like the players in Britain, received contracts and letters of intent and we had them examined legally on our behalf. The game was undergoing enormous change and we needed to know what was happening.

Naturally, we appreciate the efforts of the I.R.F.U. to

meet our needs. At the end of the 1994-95 season we received approximately £5,000 each, before tax, from sponsorship and promotional deals. The Players' Trust Fund actually topped £120,000. It works on a system where the pool of money at the end of the season is divided into 22 units, which is made up of 15 players on the field and the six replacements, with one additional unit added on behalf of the I.R.F.U.'s Charitable Trust.

With Ireland playing eight games in the championship and World Cup the figure eight was then multiplied by 22. A player who played in all eight games or who sat on the bench received 8/176ths of the total sum in the Trust. For the time and effort invested in last season by the Irish players, we were still looking at small change however.

The I.R.F.U.'s accounts make for much more impressive reading. The union's overall net assets are £22 million, according to this year's accounts, and the match income from the two home Five Nations games at Lansdowne Road has doubled in the last two years, mainly due to increased television revenue. The £2 million home International is on its way! That is big money.

A lot of the I.R.F.U.'s money last year went to clubs and branches in development projects. The cost of squad sessions in preparation for the championship and the World Cup was £180,000 which, admittedly, is a steep rise on spendings on the Irish squad in the past, but the I.R.F.U. can afford it. Without the players, after all, there would be no International games.

The I.R.F.U. has a working group looking into the building of a new ground. Lansdowne Road has been left far behind Twickenham and Murrayfield, in recent years, and the union cannot afford to start throwing its money away even though it is reportedly one of the richest unions in Europe.

The I.R.F.U. still has to move with the changing times, and that is going to be a costly business in the years to come. With increasing television money and more sponsorship, however, there should be no need for the I.R.F.U. to lose an arm or a leg in meeting the needs of its players.

The changes in the game could possibly see the movement of the Five Nations championship to the Spring and early Summer. There is no doubt but that the game of rugby, which is played on harder ground and beneath blue skies, can only help northern hemisphere countries to become effective against the likes of Australia and New Zealand in the future. We too can learn to play fast, expansive rugby all the time if we move the championship forward by a few months.

Talk of playing the championship on a home and away basis, thereby doubling the number of matches and enabling the game's marketing people to double their revenue, could also make a lot of sense. Whether the likes of Romania and Italy should be invited into the Five Nations is another interesting question. Certainly, Italy have come on enormously in recent years and would add to the intrigue and excitement of the championship.

Within Ireland, there are also tough questions to be asked and quickly answered in the times ahead. If there is to be a real future for provincial rugby in Ireland, for instance, then teams will have to receive a lot more time and attention. Now that Munster, Ulster and Leinster are competing in a new European League this season against teams from France, Wales, Romania and Italy the players in question will have to seriously devote themselves to their province, at the expense of their clubs.

The club in Ireland, I have to say, is going to be the loser in the future. Clubs will have to lose their best players for 95% of the season. The top players will have to spend almost all their time with a provincial team and a national team if they are to maintain their sharpness and quality of performance throughout the season.

As things stood in Ireland, I had no terrific interest in playing for Leinster. But with Leinster now included in a European League, and with teams from England and Scotland also joining the League next season, playing for the province will be a whole new and far more exciting ball game. Our own provincial series was no longer competitive and it was doing more harm than good to the top players in the country. Top players need top quality rugby all year around. And if Ireland is to be serious about playing rugby and wants to seriously improve, then that is how it must be! Players can not have three or four different masters, and they can not be running over and back between three or four different teams.

As it was, provincial rugby in Ireland had become boring and meaningless but, in the future, playing for Leinster or Munster or whoever could become incredibly exciting and rewarding.

In Ireland, the clubs and the provinces were trapped in mediocre situations (Connacht and the Exiles remain trapped and, for the good of their players, something must be done to offer them a more meaningful existence in the near future). The standard of the game at both club and provincial levels is very poor. There is the occasional exciting and passionate club game but, even then, the quality of the rugby on view is pretty dismal compared to rugby at any level overseas. The All-Ireland League did come to the game's aid five years ago. It has an attractive divisional structure but, in reality, there are too many senior teams in Ireland and a shortage of good players.

The clubs and provinces in Ireland, in recent years,

have not been able to do anything to help the International player. They just gave him matches which took up his time and, while that judgement may appear harsh, there are very few Irish players who privately disagree with me.

Irish clubs and provincial teams did not serve as stepping stones to the International game, and that was the great pity! That was also the great problem with Irish rugby for far too long but, now, provincial rugby can serve the Irish team in the near future.

One or the other, either the club or the province, had to be allowed to develop into well organised and professionally-minded teams. In my opinion, the province can serve Irish rugby best at this time, but they must first be developed and remodelled until they are almost unrecognisable.

The bottom line is that Irish clubs are going to have to lose their top players sooner or later. They will not have their International player for training or for the vast majority of matches, and the situation will have to be as it has been in Australia for a long time, where the International player returns to his club to play three or four matches in the entire season.

I know that sounds hard on the more ambitious clubs, and those clubs with long and proud traditions, but that is the way it must be if the game in Ireland is to be stopped from disappearing into a giant hole.

The I.R.F.U. has to see to it that the face of the game in this country is dramatically changed. It is up to the union to gather together about 100 of the country's top players and get them concentrating on provincial rugby and the Irish team, and only those two teams! The union has to inform the clubs that that is the way it has to be from now on.

As it is, Ireland is falling further and further behind the English game. We do not have a sufficiently high level of competition. Our clubs and provinces, as they are, would not live with the top English teams on a week in, week out basis.

In Scotland, there is a similar player-base to Ireland, but they possess far greater organisation. At national level, former coach Ian McGeechan set superb standards for the whole country in the late 80s and early 90s. Since the mid-80s, the Scottish union has been very sharp and they have been taking top class players with Scottish backgrounds from the English league on a consistent basis. Scotland can attract those players. Ireland, unfortunately, is not so attractive!

We have Micks and Paddys, and the sons of Micks and Paddys, playing top level rugby throughout the English leagues, but those players are told they have to go through the Irish system if they want to qualify for the national team. The only exception in recent years was the Australian, Brian Smith, who was handed the green number 10 shirt far too quickly!

Normally, the English-based player wanting to qualify for Ireland has to go through the Exiles team. There he finds the level of competition staid. That too may sound harsh, but it is true and we have to accept that. And do something about it!

The Kyran Brackens in England are asked to prove themselves in a lower level of competition than they are used to. They become disinterested. They think that their careers are going in the wrong direction, and it certainly looks like that! Paul Burke, who played on the Irish team for the first time last season, gave up a good, young career in England to come over here and try his luck. He has done well, but it has been hard for him to adjust.

What Ireland needs are two or three full-time people in England meeting players and recruiting them. After that, it is no use throwing them into our provincial series. They should ideally step from one level of competition in England to a similar level of competition in Ireland. Phelim McLoughlin and John O'Driscoll have been doing a good job in England in the recent past, but they are working on a voluntary basis. Their work is fiercely time-consuming and England is too big.

Irish rugby has a lot of hard decisions to make. I am one of those players who is already into the second-half of his career and I and members of the present Irish team, do not have that much to gain in personal terms from sweeping changes throughout the game in Ireland.

But if Ireland does not awaken to what is happening in world rugby then we can forget about playing the likes of Australia and the All Blacks in the future. We can stop thinking about beating England now and again, and instead we can think of playing Italy and Spain and their likes for the next 10 or 20 years. In the second or third division of world rugby, Ireland can be as happy as Larry, but in my opinion it will be very sad if that is where we are to be found a decade from now.

Any player who is serious about his rugby wants to play at the highest level possible. That is the most natural desire there is on the part of any athlete in any sport. If the game in Ireland is to go backwards then why should our best players want to remain in the country? They are not going to stay put. Talented teenagers are going to be on their way to England and elsewhere where they can further test themselves and explore their own capabilities.

The day when the best Irish players might be found on rugby pitches in England, France and the southern hemisphere all year around might not be all that far away, if the I.R.F.U. is not very careful.

We have to try to make Irish rugby, from head to toe, a more attractive and competitive show. We must make that effort. In more recent years it has been soul-destroying at times playing for Ireland against professional outfits like Australia and New Zealand, and England!

Last Summer, the day before the Irish team set off for the World Cup finals in South Africa, the I.R.F.U. set out its stall on the question of amateurism. The International Board had asked unions to present policy documents. It was clear, in May of 1995, that Ireland wished to run a million miles from the very thought of professionalism. The union feared for the future of the old game. The incredible pressures on players were acknowledged, but the union's thoughts on tackling those pressures was to reduce the number of International matches played in a 12 months period, to reduce the preparation period prior to Internationals and to lessen the number of squad sessions.

The I.R.F.U., therefore, was advocating that Ireland should go in the exact opposition direction to Australia and New Zealand and the big boys. The only friends and playmates we would have left, if we went down that wrong road, would be Italy and Spain and the small boys. And even some of them might not have wanted to stick around for very long in our company.

The I.R.F.U. did not acknowledge at that time that there was a pretty big battle underway for world rugby. A battle which included heavyweights like Murdoch and Packer, and a battle which, back in April, had rugby league bravely turning itself inside-out and shedding its past. Rugby league was willing to forget all about 100 years of great matches and happy times in small towns in the north of England in order to become a strong, global game. Clubs were told they might cease to exist, and they were told they could not complain! The blueprint was murderous in many respects, but in a changing and developing sports world it was considered necessary for the survival of rugby league.

In June of 1995, officials from Australia, New Zealand and South Africa announced they were handing media king Rupert Murdoch exclusive rights to rugby union in the southern hemisphere for the next 10 years in exchange for £340 million.

The deal covered a home and away series of six test matches, and a new provincial tournament, the Super 12, including five teams from New Zealand, four from South Africa and three from Australia. The Super 12 replaced the old Super 10 and ruled out Pacific Island teams like Western Samoa. It was a tough, business-like decision, and obviously sensitivity and reverence for the past did not enter into their discussions.

I am not saying that we have to be quite so brutal in these parts in which we play the old game. But we have to be hard-nosed about what needs to be done, and we have to at least be brutally honest with ourselves. In Ireland we have to shake ourselves and bite a few bullets in order to remain a dot on the overall picture of world rugby.

We do not want that dot to disappear entirely, do we?

If the three big boys in the southern hemisphere did not do what they had to do, then vast chunks or possibly even entire teams might have been lost to rugby league or a professional circus once the World Cup had ended. Once rugby league proposed making a leap into the future, then rugby union had to do likewise, though rugby union would have done it anyhow, sooner or later.

In Ireland, it is the same story as the game worldwide. We have more to lose by remaining in the past than by stepping into the future. Ireland had become a small, stagnant rugby pool. The game was going nowhere fast.

Old-fashioned beliefs and values were killing rugby in Ireland in my opinion. Slowly killing the old game.

Last August, after three days of meetings in Paris, the International Board finally, and thankfully, declared that rugby union would no longer fight off the tentacles of professionalism. I think most people associated with the game and, those people who knew what had been taking place in the southern hemisphere and elsewhere, breathed a sigh of relief.

At the Paris talks, the I.R.F.U. president, Syd Millar, and Tom Kiernan did not support all the changes which were on the table but, when reporting on the meeting later back in Dublin, they insisted that the I.R.F.U. would do its utmost in order to remain one of the major unions in the game. That is all the I.R.F.U. can be asked to do.

That's all the Irish players have ever wanted. That has been our wish for years. We wanted rugby in Ireland to do all in its power to enable us to compete against the greatest teams.

Let us get stuck into the future!

CHAPTER 14

ONE OF LIFE'S PROPS

I have an old Tracey Chapman music tape which has travelled the world with me since I first played rugby for Ireland, and possibly even before then. Only on the mornings of International matches do I listen to it. I get onto the team coach, and take the same seat I always take, next to the window down near the back. Everybody else on the Irish team knows not to sit next to me. I have the tape in my walkman. I put on the earphones and wait to be slowly carried towards Lansdowne Road, Ellis Park, Twickenham or wherever. I feel all alone on that journey. Me against the world! Naturally, it is not a very enjoyable journey.

Tracey Chapman is a black American singer who usually dwells on hard times and tough situations in her songs. The first time I listened to her tape I knew it fitted my pre-match mood perfectly. Sometimes, life is no fun.

It's no fun being imprisoned on a team coach and being carried to a stadium full of 50,000 or 60,000 people. It might look a great life from the outside, but on the coach, quietly sitting there, saying nothing, I am literally churning up inside.

All morning, I will not have eaten much. How can you have an appetite for breakfast when it honestly feels like it might be your last meal ever? We will have done some lineout practice earlier, either in the empty stadium or somewhere private, just to get all our calls exactly right one last time. Back in the team hotel, I will have turned down a light bite to eat around midday. I'll have tried to stuff down three or four bananas, and I will be on about my tenth cup of coffee. But, all morning, all I will have wanted was to get on the team coach and get to the stadium.

Then, I'm on the coach, just me and Tracey Chapman, the pair of us feeling all depressed.

That is the way I like to have it on the morning and the afternoon of a match. Life is a bitch! That's the view I want to take. The funny thing is, of course, I would not give this life up for anybody. I love it. And I even quite like the hatred I feel on the day of the match, if you can understand what I mean?

This is what I have always wanted to do, play for Ireland! At the last count I believe I have now played for Ireland 33 times and I still love it as much as I did that first time back in November, 1989 when the All Blacks were in Dublin.

That churning feeling in my stomach and the mounting anticipation is part of my life now. I accept it. In the hours before the match, it is a bit like taking a roller-coaster ride to the stadium instead of a high-seated luxury coach. No wonder I get physically sick in the dressingroom half of the time.

I do not mind getting physically sick (though I do not

love it!), because the act tells me I want to get out there and play for Ireland, and that I want to do Ireland proud.

It's still funny. In years to come, when I have retired from the Irish team, I will probably crave to return to the morning of an International match as a player and listen to Tracey Chapman's voice one more time. I will also miss the sickness.

When I have those earphones on, it is so easy to forget that it is only a game of rugby I am heading towards. It's not really life or death. And when we talk about professionalism and argue over the course which the game is now taking, we also forget!

The game is still the same. It is the same great game, and it is greater than anyone or any group of people. It is greater than Australia, South Africa and the All Blacks put together. It is far greater than the richest television mogul in the world. The fact that big business and rugby are standing at the altar together at this time does not detract from the brilliance and perfection of the game itself.

Rugby is fantastic. It has everything, power and beauty, savagery and sophistication, everything! I think it is the greatest game in the world.

I honestly feel it is a game more naturally suited to man than any other ball game. The first game of rugby I played, all those years ago in Brook House in Dublin when I was seven years old, I thought it was so exciting.

And I still feel that excitement today. Even though I'm only a prop. Actually, the prop has the best of it on the rugby pitch in my opinion. He is always in the thick of things. He sees more of the ball than anybody else, even though he does not always get his hands on it, but that is an entirely different story and one I hope I have fairly recounted in this book.

What makes me happiest? In my life there are many

things which make me happy, I must admit, but squatting down with a bunch of fat and smelly creatures every Saturday afternoon and preparing to bang head-first into another herd of the same creatures is right up there at the top of my list, or very close to it. Whether it is in England or in Ireland. Rachel and my family obviously come first.

The first scrum of every single match is a most interesting and satisfying experience. In that first scrum, you can never know for sure what is going to happen. Always in that very first scrum you have to prove yourself and prove something to your opponent. It is always hard and punishing. It's good! It's great actually. That first scrum is like your first scrum ever. It's like you versus the unknown. It's like the first and last scrum of your life.

I have two or three more years left, I sincerely hope, as one of life's props.